Simon & Schuster
Modular Science
Key Stage 4

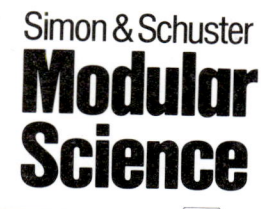

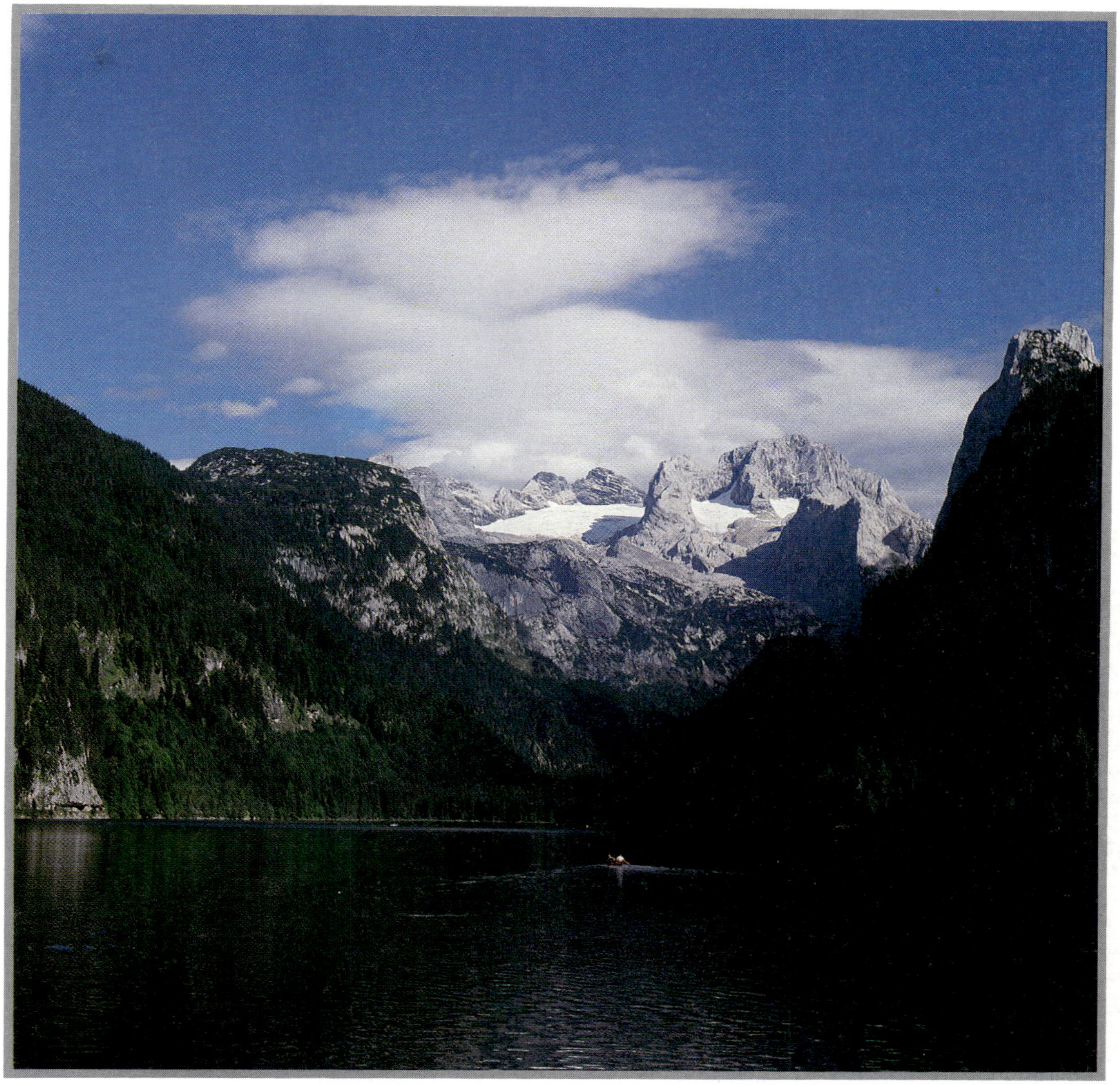

Earth, Atmosphere and Space

James Bradberry

Acknowledgements

The author and publishers would like to thank the following for permission to reproduce photographs:

Allsport/Vince Cavataio 19.1; Ashmolean Museum Oxford 5.1; British Geological Survey/NERC 3.2; The J Allan Cash Photo Library 18.1, 18.3; De Beers Consolidated Mines 4.1; Edu-Kit Productions 22.4; Geoscience Features 8.4 (J Wooldridge), 17.1, 21.2; Michael Holford 30.6; Eric Kay 8.1, 9.3, 10.2, 10.4; Lick Observatory 29.1a-g; NASA 22.1a, 23.1(ii), 23.1(iii), 26.6, 26.7, 27.1, 27.3, 27.4, 27.5, 30.2, 30.5; Natural History Museum 7.3; Novosti 31.1, NPA 22.1b; Royal Observatory Edinburgh/Anglo-Australian Telescope Board 30.4; Science Photo Library cover, 12.3 (David Parker), 20.3 (Peter Ryan), 23.1(i), 26.8 (USGS), 26.9 (USGS Flagstaff), 28.3 (George East), 31.2 (Julian Baum); South American Pictures 6.2 (Peter Ryley); Graham Topping 25.1; USGS 8.2, 16.5 (E H Bailey); USTTA 2.2.

Text © James Bradberry 1992
Design and artwork © Simon & Schuster Education 1992
Photographs © The sources credited

All rights reserved

First published in 1992 in Great Britain by
Simon & Schuster Education
Campus 400, Maylands Avenue
Hemel Hempstead, Herts HP2 7EZ

British Library Cataloguing in Publication Data
Bradberry, James
    Earth, atmosphere and space.
    4
    1. Earth sciences
    I. Title
    550
ISBN 0 7501 0174 1

Designed, typeset and illustrated by
Ian Foulis & Associates
Saltash
Cornwall
Printed in Hong Kong by Wing King Tong Co. Ltd

Key to icons used in text
IT
CP   computer program
WP   word processor
DTP desktop publishing
Safety
G   goggles

Preface

This book is written to help you understand more about the Earth and some of the processes that have influenced its development and change over the last 4500 million years.

A knowledge of the Earth and its atmosphere and space is an important part of National Curriculum Science and this book covers the Attainment Targets 9 and 16 on Earth, Atmosphere and Space in the National Curriculum.

The main requirement for becoming an Earth scientist is to be inquisitive and curious about what you can see in your environment. All the clues about the natural processes that have formed our planet are there – in the soil, rocks, seas, rivers, beaches, in the sky and in outer space. Hopefully, reading this book will encourage you to look for them yourself and find out more about them.

I hope that you will not only enjoy reading this book, but that you will find the exercises and activities interesting. More than anything I hope that it will help you to appreciate and respect the Earth of which we ourselves form a part.

James Bradberry, 1991
Withywood School, Bristol

Contents

Unit 1 The planet Earth	4	
Unit 2 How volcanoes affect us	6	
Unit 3 Volcanic activity and the landscape	8	
Unit 4 Minerals and their uses	10	
Unit 5 The uses of metallic minerals	12	
Unit 6 The search for wealth	14	
Unit 7 Sedimentary rocks	16	
Unit 8 Weathering and erosion of rocks	18	
Unit 9 Metamorphic rocks	20	
Unit 10 The rock cycle	22	
Unit 11 Earth structure	24	
Unit 12 Where earthquakes happen	26	
Unit 13 Uses of earthquake shockwaves	28	
Unit 14 Earth movements	30	
Unit 15 Fold and block mountains	32	
Unit 16 Plate tectonics	34	
Unit 17 Reading the rocks	38	
Unit 18 The salty sea	40	
Unit 19 The moving sea	42	
Unit 20 Ocean floor deposits	44	
Unit 21 Water on the land	46	
Unit 22 The power of rivers	50	
Unit 23 The atmosphere	54	
Unit 24 Global weather	56	
Unit 25 Fronts and the weather	58	
Unit 26 The solar system	60	
Unit 27 Discovering the outer planets	64	
Unit 28 The Sun	66	
Unit 29 The Moon	68	
Unit 30 The universe	70	
Unit 31 Exploring space	74	
Glossary	76	
Index	81	

Unit 1
The planet Earth

Where did the Earth come from? Why is there so much water on the Earth? Why does the Earth have an atmosphere? How old is the Earth?

When Neil Armstrong saw the Earth on the American mission to the Moon, he described it as 'a beautiful jewel in space'. He saw the vivid blue of the oceans, the white reflective clouds, the white polar icecaps and the green-brown landmasses. In fact, much of what he saw was water – in its liquid, solid or gaseous form.

Where did all this water come from?

Most scientists think that the Earth and its companion planets in the solar system were born from a cloud of gas and dust known as a **nebula**, 4600 million years ago. The gas and dust condensed to form a molten ball circling the Sun. The first surface rocks on Earth were formed as the molten surface cooled. Steam erupted from volcanoes and became water vapour in the atmosphere. Further cooling allowed vast amounts of water vapour held in the atmosphere to condense to water. This collected in hollows to form the oceans.

Why does 'water' mainly exist as a liquid on the Earth?

The Earth is one of nine major planets orbiting the Sun in the solar system. It is 150 million kilometres away from the Sun. This distance is such that there is just the right amount of heat from the Sun to allow most of the surface water to exist as a liquid. If the Earth were slightly cooler, much of the water would be stored in huge polar icecaps. If it were slightly warmer, much would exist as water vapour in the atmosphere. The Earth is the only planet known to have the conditions needed to support life.

Why is there an atmosphere?

The Earth's gravity is strong enough to hold onto its present gases but lighter gases, hydrogen and helium, have been lost. On larger planets like Saturn and Jupiter, these are the main gases in the atmosphere. Why do you think this is? Smaller planets have no atmosphere at all. Why is this? Look at the *Factfile* opposite. None of the things listed happen on the Moon's surface, even though it is about the same distance from the Sun. Try answering the question posed by Figure 1.1. Much of the Moon's surface is heavily cratered. The craters are caused by meteorites which have crashed into the Moon because of the Moon's gravity. Many of the craters are millions of years old, yet we can still see them. Try to think of two reasons why they have not been destroyed.

Activity 1.1

Draw two pie-charts to illustrate the following facts about the Earth: **CP**

(a) Land 29%
    Water 71%
(b) Pacific Ocean 46%
    Atlantic Ocean 23%
    Indian Ocean 20%
    Arctic Ocean 4%
    Other seas 7%

Factfile

The atmosphere:
- filters out harmful radiation from the Sun
- protects the Earth from meteorite falls
- acts as a store for the Sun's heat
- produces storms and air movements which spread heat and moisture across the Earth's surface, so producing weather; exposure to weather causes rocks to break down and erode away.

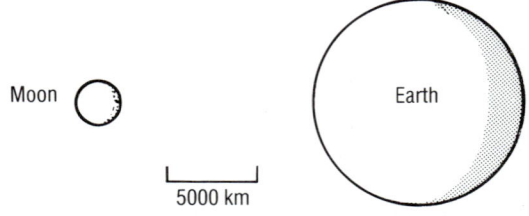

Figure 1.1 The size of the Moon in relation to the Earth. Do you think the Moon has an atmosphere? If not, why not? Why is the Moon heavily cratered while the Earth is not?

What has happened since the Earth began?

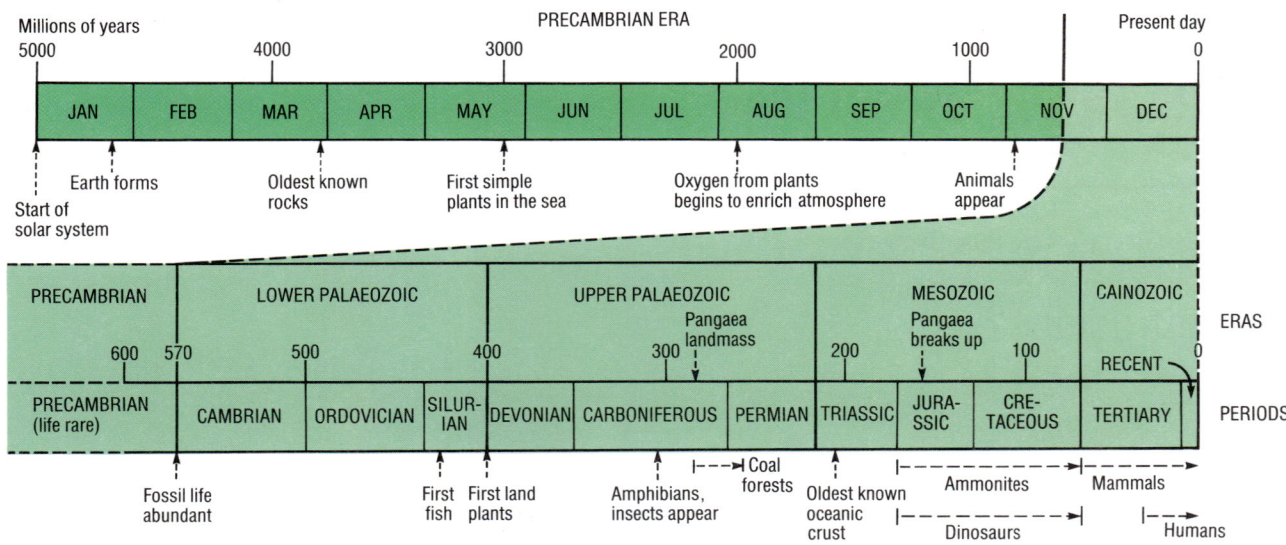

Figure 1.2 The Earth's time scale. Make a time chart like this for your classroom to show the main events in Earth history

Event	How many million years ago?
Earth forms	
First sea plants	
First animals	
Fossil life abundant	
First land plants	
Dinosaurs die out	
Humans appear	

Many events have affected the Earth during its long history. Continents have repeatedly collided and drifted apart. Mountains have been formed by folding rock layers, only to be destroyed again by the forces of weathering and erosion. All these forces are still at work today. Earthquakes and volcanoes are evidence that the continents are still on the move, carried by large slabs of rock called **plates**. Mountains are still being uplifted. The atmosphere and oceans have helped to create the environment necessary to support life.

The Earth's past history is divided into **eras**. These in turn are divided into **periods**. All the periods together represent approximately the last one-tenth of the Earth's time span (Figure 1.2). Notice how late humans appeared compared to the vast age of the Earth.

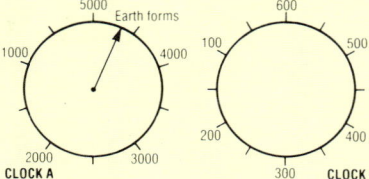

Figure 1.3 Earth-time clocks

Activity 1.2

Figure 1.2 shows Earth-time on a scale of 12 months.
1 When did the events shown above occur? Copy and complete the table.
2 Copy the circles (Figure 1.3) and use them to make two Earth-time clocks. Clock A should record the main events shown in Figure 1.2. On your copy of clock B, mark and shade in:
   a when fish appeared,
   b when amphibians appeared,
   c the differing lengths of time that dinosaurs, mammals and humans have existed.

Summary

Most of the Earth's surface is covered in water. The presence of water in its liquid state is due to the Earth receiving just the right amount of heat. The solar system formed about 5000 million years ago. Many changes have happened to the Earth since it formed about 4700 million years ago.

Questions

1 What is a nebula?
2 How long ago did the planets form?
3 Where did the Earth's water come from?
4 Why isn't there surface water on the Moon?
5 Why isn't there any weathering of rocks on the Moon?

Unit 2
How volcanoes affect us

How do volcanoes affect us? Can they change the weather? Could we use their heat energy?

What are intrusions?

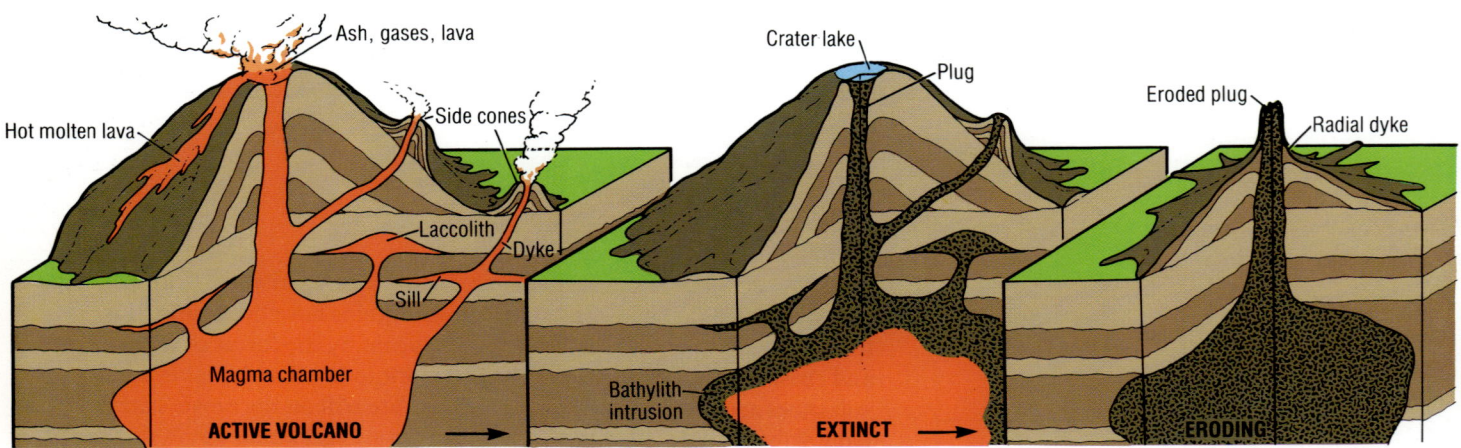

Figure 2.1 The life of a volcano

Figure 2.1 shows that underground magma does not always reach the surface to erupt as lava. Sometimes magma forces its way upwards and **intrudes** (cuts into) the surrounding rocks. A **laccolith** is a blister of magma between two layers of existing rock. **Dykes** are sheets of magma cutting across the layers – **sills** run 'with the grain' of the existing rocks. Eventually a volcano ceases all activity and the underground magma slowly cools. Given enough time, the volcano will erode away until even the dykes and sills are exposed at the surface.

Dangers of volcanoes

Active volcanoes are dangerous. Even before an eruption, the gases which are given off can make people choke to death. Ash and lava can wipe out whole towns and villages. The heat from lava can melt ice and snow. The water then mixes with fine ash to make deadly mudflows and floods. As many people drown in volcanic disasters as are killed directly by ash or lava.

Effects on climate

When huge volumes of ash are blasted high into the air, the dust can stay in the atmosphere for two or three years. When the El Chichon volcano erupted in Mexico in 1982, 550 million tonnes of ash reached a height of 38 km. High-level winds spread the cloud round the Earth. The ash blocked out some of the Sun's heat and many places recorded cooler, wetter summers in 1982/3

Figure 2.2 Old Faithful erupts every 65 minutes and the water reaches a height of 60 m

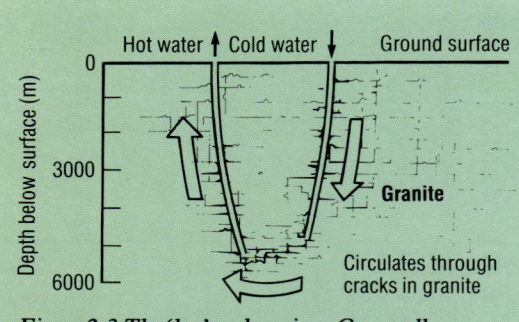

Figure 2.3 The 'hot' rock project, Cornwall

Uses of volcanic heat

Magma can heat underground rocks. Water seeping down through cracks from the Earth's surface becomes heated. Steam and gases then reach the surface, with hot springs of water and pools of boiling mud. A **geyser** is a hot-water fountain. In the Yellowstone National Park in the USA there are more than 200 geysers. Old Faithful is one example (Figure 2.2). It erupts every 65 minutes when pressure builds up in the underground rocks. In Iceland, water from hot springs is used to heat homes, swimming pools and greenhouses. Even tropical plants like bananas can be grown successfully. In New Zealand and Iceland, steam from hot springs is used to generate electricity. In Britain there are no active volcanoes but there are buried granite masses that were once magma. The rock is still hot. In Cornwall, experiments are going on to make use of this heat (Figure 2.3). Two holes are drilled and water is pumped down one hole and back up the other hole to the surface. If a well is sunk to a depth of 6 km, then water can be produced at a temperature of 210 °C. The steam can be used to generate electricity.

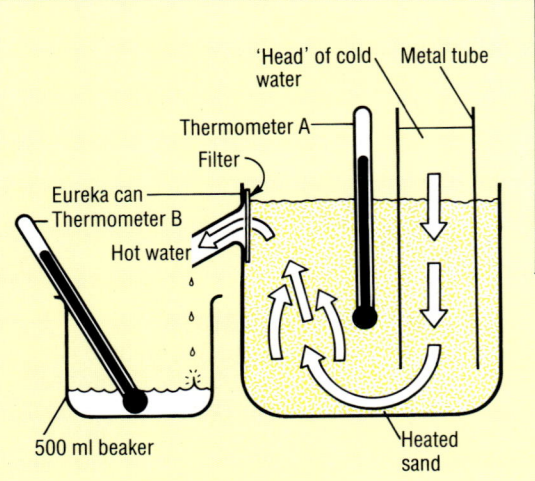

Figure 2.4 Apparatus to show how water is heated by rocks

Water volume (ml)	Temperature A (°C)	Temperature B (°C)
250		
500		
750		
1000		

Activity 2.1

How water is heated by rocks

Fill a eureka can with sand. Empty the sand into a metal dish and heat in an oven for 1 hour at about 200 °C. Transfer the warmed sand to the eureka can, with the metal tube in position as shown in Figure 2.4. Pour a litre of water into a measuring cylinder and slowly trickle 250 ml into the top of the tube. Then take readings on both thermometers. Add another 250 ml of water and measure the temperature again. Set out your results in a table like the one shown here.

1. Use your results to draw line graphs of volume against temperature. **CP**
2. What is the difference in temperature between A and B? Does this difference remain the same?
3. Do the results vary if you pour cold water in quickly? How efficient is water at removing heat from the hot sand? Explain fully what you have found out in this activity and how it relates to the hot-rock project in Cornwall.

Summary

Volcanoes can threaten human lives but they can also be useful to us. People can learn to use the Earth's heat and modern technology can be used to forecast dangerous eruptions.

Questions

1. How do volcanoes cause human deaths?
2. What are geysers? How are hot springs used?
3. Find out about four methods used to measure changes in volcanoes. Explain how each method works.
4. What are the main kinds of igneous intrusion?

Forecasting eruptions

The only way to predict an eruption is to watch a volcano carefully and note any changes taking place. It is possible to take infra-red pictures of the world's volcanoes from satellites and see if any of them are beginning to heat up. If any changes are noticed, then ground equipment can be used to study the changes more closely. An electronic thermometer, called a **thermocouple**, is used to measure temperature down to 3 m below the Earth's surface. If the temperature rises it will show that the magma is moving nearer to the surface. Many volcanoes swell slightly just before an eruption, as the magma moves upwards. Changes in slope are recorded using a kind of spirit-level called a **tiltmeter**. If these methods are used, then an eruption can be predicted. The difficulty is knowing exactly what day and how big the eruption will be.

Unit 3
Volcanic activity and the landscape

How do rocks form out of molten material? Are there any British volcanoes? How has volcanic activity affected British scenery?

Rocks which form out of molten material are called **igneous** rocks. They form as lava cools at the surface, or as magma cools below ground. When molten material cools it forms crystals and eventually they combine to make solid rock.

Activity 3.1
Discuss in groups.
Would magma cool faster above or below ground? How would the rate of cooling affect the size of the crystals?

Activity 3.2
1 Examine a piece of basalt lava using a hand lens. You should be able to see the interlocking crystals.
  - What do the crystals look like?
  - Would you describe the crystal size as 'fine', 'medium' or 'coarse'?
2 Examine a piece of granite. Using the size of the crystals as a guide would you say that this rock had formed at the surface or below ground?
3 Examine a piece of obsidian. Why are there no crystals?

Activity 3.3
How igneous rocks form
Label two boiling tubes A and B. One-third fill both tubes with naphthalene flakes. Gently heat tube A until the flakes melt. Then quickly wrap it in tin foil to keep it warm and stand it upright in a beaker. Melt the naphthalene in tube B. Then cool it rapidly by standing it in water in another large beaker.
1 Look carefully at the solid naphthalene in each tube. What differences can you see?
2 Which of the tubes represents what happens when basalt and granite solidify?

What about British volcanoes?

It might seem surprising to be talking about volcanoes in Britain. The truth is that at one time there were a great number of them. Now they are all extinct. Figure 3.1 is a map of where volcanic and intrusive rocks can be found in the British Isles. The events which produced them happened at different times in Britain's history – millions of years ago. In many places volcanic rocks have produced some impressive scenery. In Northern Ireland there is a large area of plateau basalt. Layer after layer of basalt was erupted from long cracks called **fissures**, to form a flat upraised plateau. These are still found today in places like Iceland. The Giant's Causeway in County Antrim (Figure 3.2) is part of the basalt plateau. Notice the basalt columns or pillars. These were formed as the layers of basalt lava cooled and contracted. The shrinkage caused by the cooling has made the rocks crack into vertical columns (see Activity 3.4).

How many sides do the columns have? Why did people invent the legend that giants used to cross here from Scotland to Ireland?

Activity 3.4
Add clay powder to water until you have a sloppy mixture. Then pour into a shallow tray. Fill to a depth of no more than 4 mm. Leave the tray to dry out slowly in a warm place, eg over a radiator.
1 Explain what happens to the layer of mud as it dries out.
2 In this case, what causes the mud layer to contract as it dries?

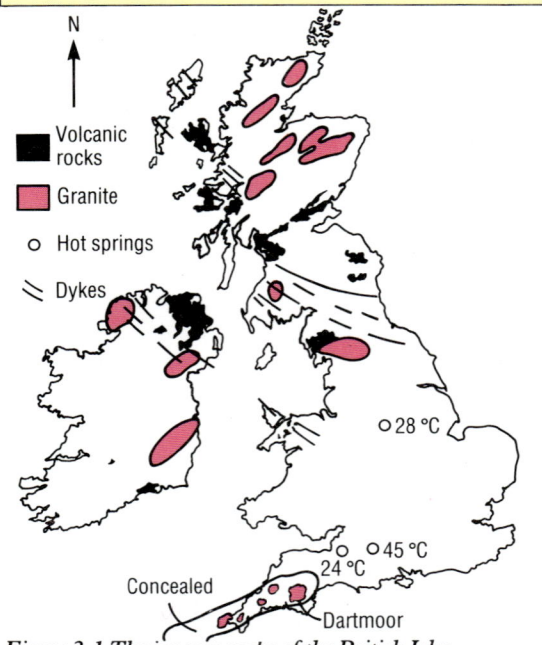

Figure 3.1 The igneous rocks of the British Isles

Figure 3.2 Giant's Causeway, County Antrim. How many sides does each column have?

> ### Activity 3.5
> Examine a piece of dolerite. Then discuss in groups and answer the following questions.
> 1. Would the Whin Sill have cooled more slowly or more quickly than basalt?
> 2. Why did the Romans happen to choose this feature for their wall?
> 3. What landscape feature would you expect to see where the River Tees crosses the Whin Sill?

In addition to the lava flows and volcanoes, there are also many dykes and sills, especially in the North of the British Isles. When erosion removes the overlying rocks, dykes and sills often form ridges and hills because they are harder and do not wear away as quickly. Part of Hadrian's Wall is built on a sill intrusion. This is a thick sheet of **dolerite** called the Whin Sill. It is sandwiched between softer sedimentary rock layers. Dolerite is a rock like basalt but it has bigger crystals.

The remnants of old volcanoes can be found in many places throughout Britain. Mount Snowdon is not a volcano as such, but the whole mountain is made of layers of ash and lava that came from a distant volcanic vent. In other places, large granite masses have cooled below ground, to be later exposed by erosion, eg Dartmoor in South-West England. Hot springs are found in at least three places. The effect of igneous activity on scenery can be seen along many of our coastlines. Figure 3.3 shows how a coastline is formed as the waves erode hard and soft rocks at different rates.

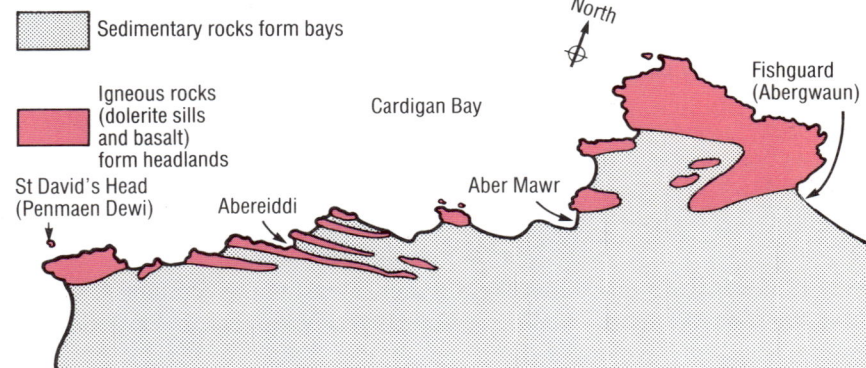

Figure 3.3 Hard and soft rocks erode at different rates as they are attacked by waves

Summary

British volcanoes all became extinct millions of years ago, but lavas and igneous intrusions have made their mark and are still visible as part of our scenery.

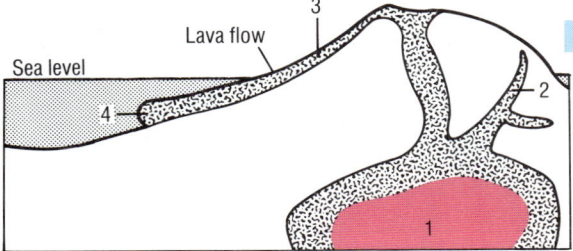

Figure 3.4 Four different cooling environments

Questions

1. Look at Figure 3.4. Write down the numbers 1–4. Next to each number put the correct description for the grain size – large/medium/fine crystals or glass.
2. Explain why rates of cooling will be different in each case.
3. Name the igneous structures at 1 and 2.
4. What is columnar jointing? Explain fully how this structure forms.
5. List all the new words you have come across in the last two units. Then design a crossword with a set of clues. (WP)

Unit 4
Minerals and their uses

Nearly all of the things you use every day – fuel, tools, clothes, food – have come, directly or indirectly, from minerals.

What is a mineral?

The rocks of the Earth are made up of minerals. A mineral is a naturally formed non-living substance with its own structure, shape and chemical make-up. Over 2000 minerals are known, but most rocks are formed from seven mineral groups.

What is an element?

Each mineral is made of one or more **element**. An element is a substance that cannot be broken down chemically any further. Sometimes a mineral is made of just one element. Gold is both an element and a mineral; diamond (Figure 4.1) is made of the single element carbon. There are about 100 known elements but only eight are very common (see Figure 4.2).

Compounds

Many minerals are compounds of one or more elements, eg common salt is a compound of sodium and chlorine. Quartz is a compound of silicon and oxygen. It is found in many rocks.

Where do minerals occur?

A mineral ore is any useful mineral substance that is worth the time, money and effort to remove from the Earth. Most metallic ores form crystals in cooling magma or in hot watery solutions. They crystallize out at different temperatures as can be seen in Figure 4.3.

Although many minerals are rock-formers, they are also found in mineral **veins** (Figure 4.4). A vein is a fissure (crack) in the rocks through which hot watery fluids can pass. Hot fluids circulate through the fissures above a heat source such as a granite intrusion, carrying dissolved minerals. Crystals of different minerals grow on the walls of the vein. There are many mineral veins in Cornwall, surrounding the intruded granites. As the granite has cooled, hot metallic solutions above the granite mass have moved upwards through cracks in the nearby rock.

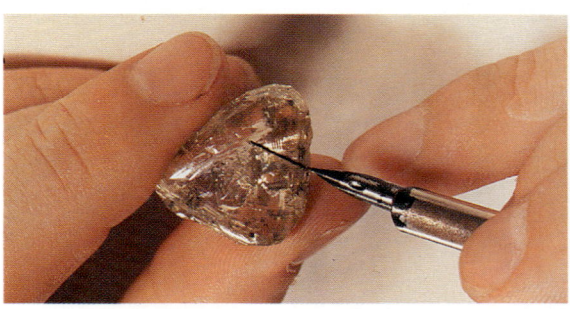

Figure 4.1 A diamond is marked before cutting

Element	Percentage (%)
Oxygen	47
Silicon	28
Aluminium	8
Iron	5
Calcium	3.5
Sodium	3
Potassium	2.5
Magnesium	2

Figure 4.2 Elements in the Earth's crust

Activity 4.1

1. Make a pie-chart of the information given in Figure 4.2. **CP**
2. How much of the Earth's crust is made of non-metallic elements?
3. Which two metals are the most plentiful?

Metallic ore	Temperature of formation (°C)
Tin	350 – 500
Copper	300 – 400
Lead	200 – 300
Zinc	200 – 300
Iron	below 200

Figure 4.3 Crystallization temperatures of different metallic ores

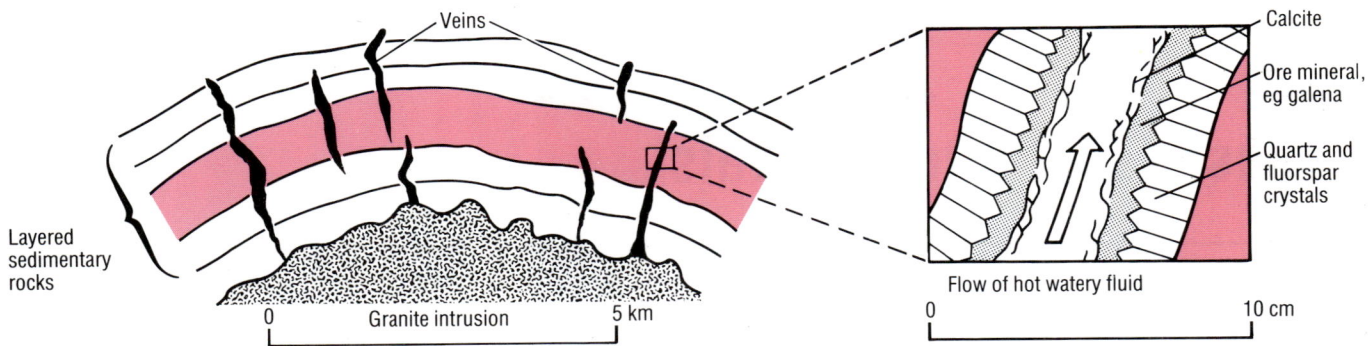

Figure 4.4 The formation of mineral veins

Activity 4.2

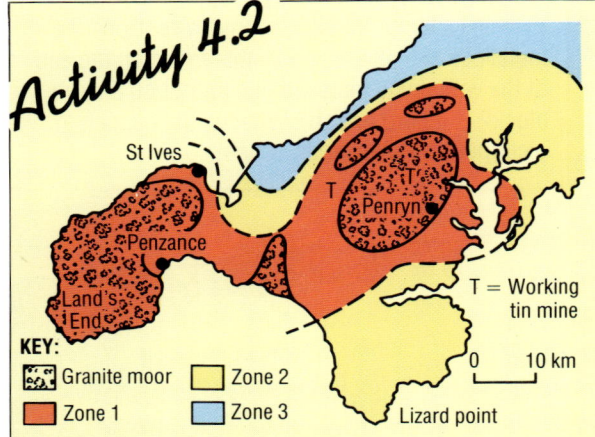

Figure 4.5 The rocks of Western Cornwall

Where should the mine be?

Imagine you are working for a mining company. They have asked you to find out the best places to mine different metal ores in Cornwall. You are given the map in Figure 4.5 which shows three different temperature zones.

1. Explain which of the three zones would have been the hottest at the time the minerals formed.
2. One of the ores is sometimes found in veins inside the granite mass. What is its name?
3. Name two metal ores found in each of zones 1 and 2, and the ore found in zone 3.
4. Copy or trace the mineral map into your book. Use a colour key to show where the following ores would be found: tin and copper, lead and zinc, iron.

More about tin mining

Cornwall has been a source of tin ore since Roman times and it is still able to provide British industry with most of the tin it needs. In the early 1980s there were eight working tin mines. The world price of the tin then collapsed and the expense of mining tin became more than the value of the metal. Only the bigger tin mines like South Crofty Mine were able to keep going. Here the worked ore comes from 16 different veins. Zinc, copper, silver and tungsten are also mined.

The uses of tin

Tin is useful because it mixes well with other metals and does not corrode easily. It is mainly used to make tinplate – a thin layer of tin is melted onto a moving sheet of steel. Tinplate is used to make tin cans because it is much cheaper than using pure tin. Tin is also added to zinc to make brass and is used in paint, wood preservatives and fungicides.

Activity 4.3

Draw a pie-chart to illustrate the following information about the uses of tin. **CP**

Uses of tin	Percentage (%)
Tinplate	55
Solder	25
Alloys (eg brass)	5
Other uses	15

Summary

Minerals are the ingredients of rocks and they also form in veins. Many minerals, especially the metallic ones, are very useful to us. A mineral ore is any mineral that is worth the time and money to extract from the ground.

Questions

1. Write down the meanings of these words: mineral, element, crust.
2. Why are many mineral-ore deposits found in places where there have been volcanoes or igneous intrusions?
3. What is a mineral ore?

Unit 5
The uses of metallic minerals

For thousands of years humans have been searching for useful minerals. Stone Age people realised they could make use of flint for tool making. Some of the earliest ores to be discovered were minerals containing copper. People found that it could be shaped into arrowheads and axe-heads much more quickly and easily than flint.

The discovery of bronze

As you have discovered in Activity 5.1, copper is a soft metal, and hence unsuitable for use in hard-wearing tools. Eventually people found a way of overcoming these problems. Tin is also a soft metal but when added to copper the combined metal or **alloy** is much harder than either of the metals on their own. The alloy of copper and tin is called **bronze**. Bronze swords and tools (Figure 5.1) were being made as early as 1500 BC.

The discovery of aluminium

Although aluminium is a plentiful metal and present in nearly every kind of rock, it is difficult to extract. The only workable ore is the mineral **bauxite** – a kind of soil. This mineral forms when aluminium-rich rocks are softened and broken down by weathering. Rain carries away the soluble parts of the weathered rock, leaving insoluble aluminium oxide behind as bauxite. Aluminium is a good conductor of electricity and is light, strong and does not corrode in air.

Activity 5.1
Properties of copper
Examine a length of thick copper wire. Does the metal bend easily? Is it possible to flatten the end of the wire if you hit it with a hammer on an iron block? Is it hard or soft? What would happen to a copper axe-head when in use?

The discovery of iron

Iron ore needs much higher smelting temperatures than either tin or copper. Its melting point is around 1500 °C. It was discovered later than copper or tin – about 3500 years ago. Again it was found that if small amounts of carbon were added to the iron it became much harder. The alloy of copper and tin is called **steel**. Steel tools contain 1.5% carbon. By 1000 BC, steel was being used in India. Imagine a battle between equal numbers of warriors with bronze swords and opponents with steel swords! Who do you think would win?

Iron is still the most widely used of all the metals. Every year the world produces around 400 million tonnes of iron. Twice that tonnage of ore has to be mined. Haematite is the most common ore.

Activity 5.2
The uses of aluminium
Make a list of all the uses of aluminium you can think of. Use encyclopedias and reference books to help you.

Specific gravity

Most metallic minerals feel much heavier than non-metallic ones. This 'heaviness' property is usually defined as the **specific gravity** – the relative density of the material compared to water. Most rocks and minerals, eg quartz, are just over 2.5 times as dense as water. Compare how heavy a hand-sized piece of quartz feels next to a metallic mineral sample like galena.

Figure 5.1

Activity 5.3

Identifying metal ores

Examine samples of the following minerals:

- chalcopyrite (copper)
- galena (lead)
- haematite (iron)
- cassiterite (tin)
- sphalerite (zinc)
- bauxite (aluminium).

Test each mineral for its **hardness** on Mohs' scale and for **streak**. The method for doing this is explained in *Earth, Atmosphere and Space 2*. Write down your results on a Record Chart (Figure 5.2). Use the chart to record the form or habit, and cleavage or fracture. The table in Figure 5.3 will help you to sort out the samples and identify them.

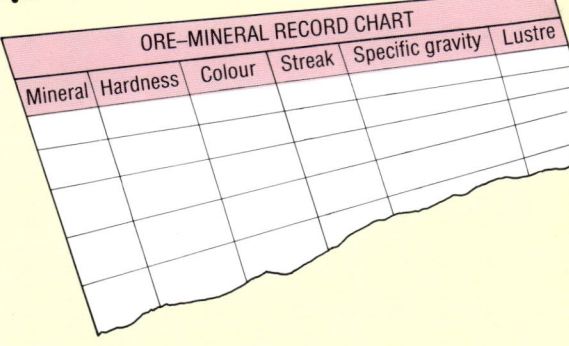

Figure 5.2 Ore-mineral record chart

Mineral	Hardness	Colour	Streak	Breakage	Specific gravity	Lustre (shininess)
Cassiterite	6–7	black or brown	pale grey	uneven	7	varies
Galena	2.5	silver grey	lead grey	small cubes	7.5	silvery
Sphalerite	4	black/brown	light brown	splits easily	4	plastic
Chalcopyrite	4	brass yellow	greenish	uneven	4	brassy
Haematite	5–6	black/red-brown	red-brown	uneven	5	metallic
Bauxite	–	grey to brown	–	–	2.5	dull

Figure 5.3 The properties of ore minerals. (Note: Because bauxite is really an aluminium-rich soil, it is not possible to give values for hardness, streak and breakage)

1. Which of these ores is the lightest/heaviest?
2. One of the minerals listed contains silver in addition to the main ore metal. Which one do you think it is? Why?

Activity 5.4

Smelting lead and zinc ores
Wear safety glasses

Put a spatula measure of powdered cerrusite (an ore of lead) or powdered sphalerite (zinc ore) in the hollow of a charcoal block. Then place the block on a gauze and tripod and strongly heat using a Bunsen flame (Figure 5.4). A blowpipe can be used to heat more strongly. Eventually a bead of metal will form. Remove the bead with tongs and examine the metal closely.

1. What kind of change took place in each case?
2. How long did both ores take to melt?

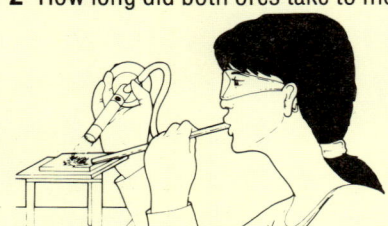

Figure 5.4 Heating cerrusite to form lead. Hold the Bunsen burner so that the flame touches the powder. Using a blowpipe, carefully blow the top of the flame directly on to the powder

Summary

People have made use of metallic minerals for centuries. Metals with low melting points were the first to be used by Stone Age people. The discovery of steel and aluminium came much later as technology developed.

Questions

1. What was the first material people used for tool making?
2. Why would people using bronze have an advantage over people using stone tools?
3. What are the two metals that make up the alloy bronze?
4. Explain why you think the use of iron was not discovered until much later in human history.
5. What element is added to iron to make steel?
6. To show the composition of steel, make a square containing 100 little squares. Then shade in the proportion of carbon squares to iron. **CP**
7. How much iron ore is mined every year?
8. What is the most common iron ore?
9. Explain how bauxite is formed and what it is used for.
10. Find out the uses of lead, zinc and copper, using your local library as a source of information. Then write a report. **WP**

Unit 6
The search for wealth

Before minerals can be taken out of the ground and used, they need to be found. How do people know where to look for valuable minerals?

Old methods

In the past, prospectors relied on their own senses to find mineral deposits. They used a forked stick like a water diviner. If there were an orebody nearby, they believed that the stick would move downwards. For many years the discovery of diamonds, gold and petroleum (oil) was really a matter of luck. Early discoveries of gold led to the famous Gold Rushes in the 1800s in North America, Africa and Australia. Prospectors would spend months of work panning for gold. They would swirl mud taken from the river bed around in a pan; they hoped to find a small lump or nugget of gold (Figure 6.2). This could lead them to a vein farther upstream from which the gold had been eroded.

What is a placer?

Although many ores form in veins near igneous rocks, erosion may wear the rocks away and move the minerals. For example, a stream cutting through rocks containing ores will wash them away. They are then deposited along with the sands and gravels on beaches and in river channels. Any mineral with a specific gravity higher than '3' quickly settles, unless the water current is very strong. Deposits of sediments that are rich in ores are called **placers**. The inner bend of a river is a likely spot.

Modern prospecting

Today the finding of ore deposits relies much more on modern technology. Satellites take detailed photographs of the Earth's surface to detect the slightest differences in the rock structure. High-detail photographs can show up mineral ores, even where there is thick forest.

Magnetic surveys
A sensitive instrument called a **magnetometer** can be towed behind an aircraft. It will quickly detect changes in magnetism caused by some orebodies. Magnetic ores will show up as peaks on the recording trace.

Gravimetric surveys
Metallic ores are usually denser than ordinary rocks and they have a slightly greater gravitational pull. They can be found by measuring tiny variations in the force of gravity using a **gravimeter**. This instrument has a very sensitive weighted spring. The amount by which the spring stretches is measured from place to place. Look at Figure 6.4, then answer the following questions.
1 Where is the pull of gravity the least? What is the cause of this?
2 How would the gravity reading show where the orebody was?

Activity 6.1

Panning for mineral ores
Panning is a technique that separates heavier ore-mineral fragments from lighter unwanted grains. This activity is messy and best done outdoors.

Use a flat-bottomed pan with sloping sides, eg a frying pan. Place some broken fragments of galena in the pan and half-fill it with damp sand and clay. Thoroughly mix the fragments with the sand and clay. Fill the pan to the brim with water and rock and turn the pan in a swirling action (see Figure 6.1). Allow the sand to slop over the edge or pour the murky water into a bucket. Top up with clean water and repeat the procedure. The galena should stay at the bottom of the pan.
1 Why does the galena stay in the pan?
2 Gold has a specific gravity of 19. Would it be lighter or heavier than galena? Would it be more or less likely than galena to stay in the pan?

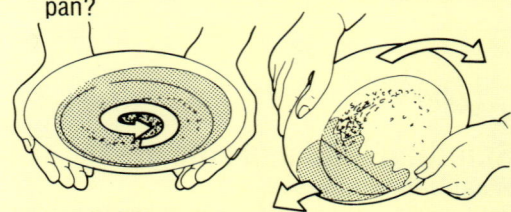

Figure 6.1 Panning for metal ores

Figure 6.2 Panning for gold

Activity 6.2

Figure 6.3 A placer deposit on a river bed. Where would the gold and galena minerals be – area A or B?

Where would the gold be?
Study Figure 6.3.
1 Why is the placer on the inner bend of the river?
2 The diagram shows two locations A and B, where galena and gold were found. In which of the two places do you think gold was found? Give your reasons.
3 On your copy of this diagram label where you would expect gold and galena to be deposited.

Seismic prospecting
Seismic prospecting is used to map out underground rock structures. An explosion or vibration sets off shockwaves, which bounce off the rock layers and can then be recorded (Figure 6.5). This can show up where the mineral deposit is.

Geochemical surveys
Soil above or near to rocks containing ores will be rich in that particular metal. So will the plants growing in the soil. Chemical analyses of the plants and soil would show what the ore is and possibly its location.

Figure 6.4 A gravimetric survey

What is its value?

After a new ore has been found, scientists will drill into it and take samples. They want to find out the size and quality of the deposit. Many ores are not mined because they are too small or too difficult to reach. To be a worthwhile ore, the value of the mineral must be *greater* than the cost of extracting it.

Summary
Nowadays it is unusual for rich deposits of oil and mineral ore to be found by accident. So how are useful minerals discovered? What are the techniques of discovery? The development of new skills and technology means that finding new minerals is not just by chance like it used to be.

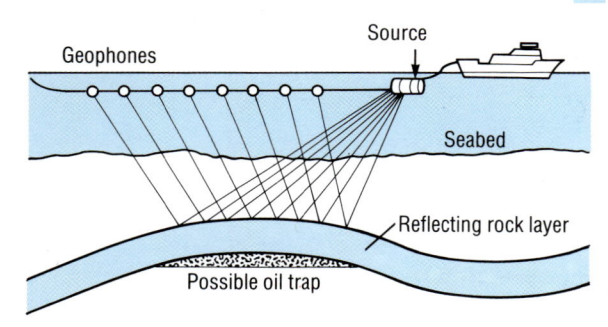

Figure 6.5 A seismic survey can see the rock structures below the seabed

Questions
1 Imagine you are a prospector who has found gold in a river in America. **WP** Write to your friend in England and give details of the panning technique. In your letter, explain what a placer is and how it has formed.
2 How have modern methods improved the chances of finding ores? Explain the main methods of ore detection.
3 The world is running out of many ores. The table shows the lifetimes of the main metal ores if they are used at present rates. Make a bar chart of the figures in the table below. **CP**

Ore	Aluminium	Copper	Iron	Lead	Tin	Zinc
Lifetime (years)	130	35	240	25	25	25

Unit 7
Sedimentary rocks

What happens to all the broken fragments of rock that are produced as the land is worn away? **Sedimentary** rocks are mainly formed from the broken fragments of previous rocks.

How are sedimentary rocks formed?

Boulders roll down mountainsides and streams carry pebbles, sand and silt to the sea. The movement of material is due to the action of running water, wind and ice-sheets. Rivers are especially effective at transporting material. The River Mississippi carries 1000 million cubic metres of sediment into the sea every year. As the river enters the sea, the current slows down. The sediment is dumped to form a huge layered mound structure called a **delta**. This has been happening for millions of years and the pile of sediment is now 17 km thick. Deltas are found at the mouths of many rivers, especially where there are few ocean currents. The river flow is often sluggish here because of all the dumped sediment. This causes the river channel to split into several smaller channels called **distributaries**. The delta steadily grows away from the original coastline as more layers of sediment are added (Figure 7.1).

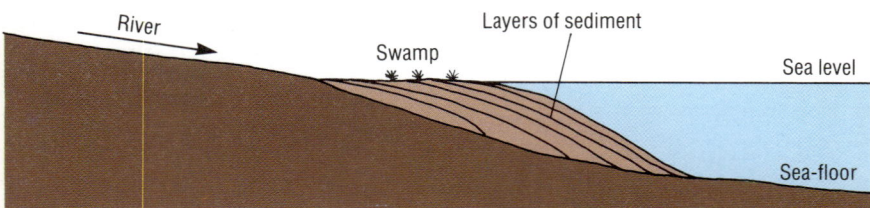

Figure 7.1 The delta extends seawards as more and more sediment is dumped

How do sand and mud become rock?

Early sediment begins to be squashed by the weight of the new material on top. Sand grains are pushed closer together – a process called **compaction**. This forces water out of the sediment. As the water moves between the grains, thin layers of calcium carbonate, silica or iron oxide are left behind on each grain as a thin coating. This **cementing** process makes the grains stick together. You can find out how both these processes work in Activity 7.1.

Types of sedimentary rock

Not all sediments are made from older rocks that have been worn away from the land surface. Many limestones are organic rocks formed from the remains of animals and plants (Figure 7.3). Layers of coal are also organic. They are the carbonized remains of trees and other plants. A third group of chemical sedimentary rocks forms when layers of minerals and salt are deposited by evaporation.

Activity 7.1

Making rocks

Rock 1: Thoroughly mix three teaspoonfuls of damp sand with one teaspoonful of clay powder. Do not add water. Use a rock-making syringe to squeeze the grains together. Then push out the sand-clay 'rock' onto paper to dry (Figure 7.2).

Rock 2: Repeat the above process, this time adding one teaspoonful of plaster of Paris to the damp sand, to act as a cementing material.

Rock 3: You could also make the rock called a **conglomerate** by mixing one teaspoonful each of dry sand, plaster of Paris and aquarium gravel together with a few drops of water.

Allow these three rocks to dry out completely and harden. This could take a few days. The rocks have been made by cementing and compacting sediments. This is how most sedimentary rocks form.

1 Examine the 'rocks' – which is the hardest? Test them with your fingernail or with a steel point to find out.
2 Look at samples of sandstone and compare them with the rocks you have made. Are they harder or softer?

(Note: Keep the samples you have made in this activity for use in Activity 8.2.)

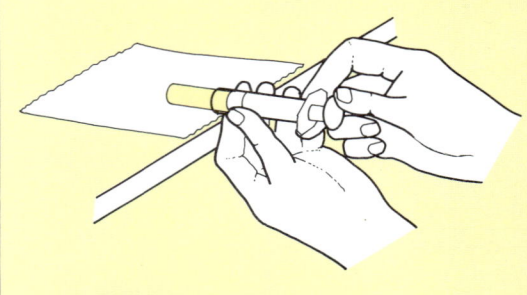

Figure 7.2 Making 'rock'

What are chemical rocks?

Most limestones are made of fragments of shells, corals and other sea creatures, but it is also possible to find limestones that have been formed directly from seawater. Calcium carbonate becomes less soluble in warm water, so it deposits (**precipitates**) as lime. The 'scale' in a kettle is a form of chemical limestone – so are stalactites in limestone caves.

Oolitic limestones

In tropical climates where warm seawater evaporates, sand grains become coated with layers of lime. Small spheres called **ooliths** are formed. Each oolith is made of a number of layers. They form on sloping shores of tropical seas where tides roll the ooliths up and down in the warm water. Finally they collect to form oolitic limestone.

Figure 7.3 Wenlock limestone. Look carefully for brachiopods, corals and bivalve shells. Notice the fine lime mud cement

Activity 7.2

Oolitic limestone
Examine a sample of oolitic limestone with a hand lens. Note the size of the spheres. All limestone reacts with acid. Put a drop of dilute hydrochloric acid on the sample of limestone. Repeat this with some scale from a kettle. Write down what happens.

Activity 7.3

Evaporating water
Try to find out what kinds of salts are left when seawater is evaporated. Heat seawater in an evaporating dish. Do the same with river water and distilled water for comparison.
1 Which kind of water leaves the most deposit?
2 Look at samples of halite and gypsum and write down what they are like – their colour, hardness, etc.

What are evaporites?

These are sediments formed when water evaporates and precipitates its dissolved chemicals. This can happen in a hot dry climate on the edge of a shallow sea. Lime is the first sediment to form, followed by other salts such as gypsum and halite (rock salt) (see Figure 7.4).

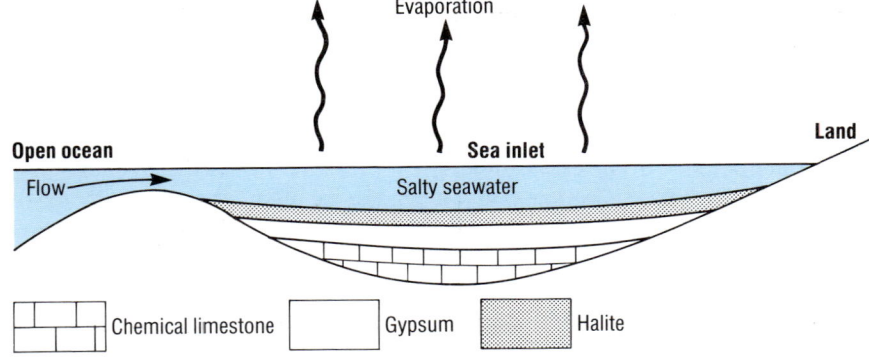

Figure 7.4 Evaporites

Questions
1 What is a delta? How does it form?
2 Explain how a sloppy sand becomes rock. **WP**
3 What are the three types of sedimentary rock?
4 What kind of sedimentary rock is coal?
5 How does oolitic limestone form?
6 What are evaporites? How do they form?

Summary

Most eroded rock fragments are deposited in layers to form new sedimentary rocks. There are different rock types according to how and where they have formed.

Unit 8
Weathering and erosion of rocks

When an earthquake turned a bridge to rubble in San Francisco in 1989, or when Mt St Helen's volcano blew up a mountainside in 1980, it was clear to everyone that natural forces can change the Earth. These are dramatic changes, but there are also much slower quieter changes happening, taking thousands of years. These changes are caused by the way rocks react to the weather. They are known as the forces of **weathering** and **erosion**. Figure 8.1 shows a frost-shattered boulder in Greenland. How do natural forces cause this kind of damage?

What happens to rocks?

Weathered rocks are usually much softer than 'fresh' unweathered rocks because the original mineral structures have been slowly destroyed. Therefore they are worn down much more quickly by water, ice, wind and wave action. The wearing-down process is called erosion. There are two main processes at work in weathering: **disintegration** and **decomposition**. Disintegration is the breaking apart of rocks by physical forces; decomposition is the decay (rotting) of rocks as they react chemically to the action of water and oxygen. Water dissolves many rock minerals and the rock is softened.

Disintegration: frost action

The processes involved in weathering vary with the climate. In mountainous regions where it is wet and cold, frost action is the main kind of weathering. Water freezes in cracks and expands as it turns to ice. Ice takes up 9% more space than the same amount of water. Therefore the freezing process puts rocks on either side of the crack under great pressure – 140 kg per square centimetre. The crack is widened and when the ice melts, there is room for even more water to collect and the process repeats itself. This process of frost shattering loosens rocks and they fall down slopes to collect as scree.

What is exfoliation?

In hot deserts, direct heating of rocks by the Sun, followed by cooling at night, makes the minerals expand and contract at different rates. This sets up immense stresses in the rocks and they crack and break up. Even in deserts, water soaks into the cracks from the dew created each night by the rapid cooling. This helps the weathering process, which mostly affects the outer layers of rocks. They peel off and break away to expose new fresh rock to the same process. This is called **exfoliation** (Figure 8.2).

Activity 8.1

Breaking a sugar lump
There are two ways to break up a sugar lump.
1. What happens to the sugar lump if you press down on it with a spoon? This is a physical process.
2. Another way to break up the sugar is to stand it in a saucer of warm water. What happens to the lump?

When you add a sugar lump to a hot drink and stir, you are crushing it with a spoon and dissolving it at the same time. The same is true with the weathering of rocks. Both disintegration and decomposition act together to break down the rock.

Figure 8.1 A frost-shattered boulder in Greenland

Figure 8.2 Exfoliation at Half Dome, Yosemite, California

Activity 8.2

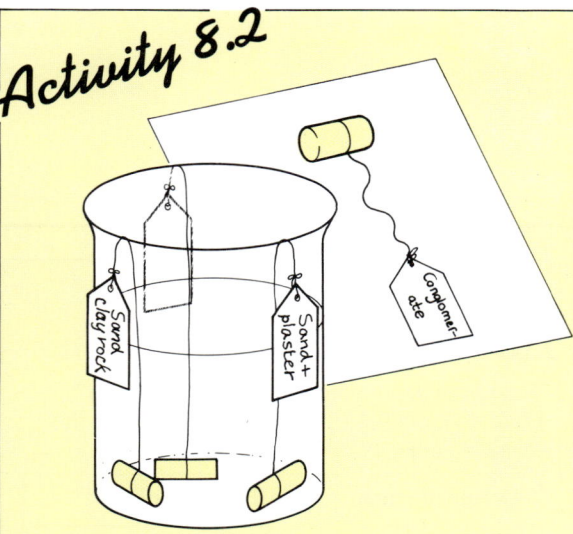

Figure 8.3 How long does it take for rocks to crumble in water?

Chemical weathering by water

Over many years, the minerals in rocks and the cementing material holding the rock grains together may be dissolved by water. Streams then carry the dissolved material to the sea.

In Activity 7.1 you made three rocks from sediments using different cementing materials. How will water affect these 'rocks'?

Tie a piece of cotton thread around each of the three rock samples and lower them into a beaker half filled with cold water. Watch the rocks to see if they begin to crumble (Figure 8.3). Leave any which do not crumble and look at them the following day. If they still have not crumbled, remove them and allow them to dry out thoroughly. Then put them back in the water for a day or so. Repeat this several times.

1. Which rock is the first to crumble?
2. Which rock resists weathering the most?
3. Record the time it takes for each rock to crumble. Show these results in a bar chart.
4. Why did some rocks crumble more easily?

CP

How rocks decompose: chemical weathering

Some rocks can be broken down slowly by water alone as minerals react with rainwater. Limestone contains calcium carbonate. This reacts with the slightly acid rainwater, turning it into the soluble calcium bicarbonate. Cracks in the limestone are widened and caves are formed. Limestone caves may contain a mass of stalactites and stalagmites (Figure 8.4). They are formed from dripping water that seeps through the cave.

Figure 8.4 Stalagmites and stalactites

Activity 8.3

Work in pairs

If possible, use a cassette recorder for this activity. Imagine that you are to appear on the radio. You have been asked to explain fully all you know about the scene in Figure 8.1. Get your friend to note down or tape what you say. Then reverse the process and get your friend to do the same with the scene in Figure 8.2. The transcripts could then be written up. **WP**

Activity 8.4

How does water act on rock?

How could you test whether limestone caves are formed by the action of water? Place a small piece of limestone in a test tube and two-thirds fill with water. Do the same with another test tube and fill with water and hydrochloric acid. What changes do you see happening?

Summary

Rocks at the Earth's surface break up and decay in the processes of weathering and erosion. Many examples of these processes can be seen in exposures of bare rock, and on buildings and gravestones.

Questions

1. Take photos or sketches of local examples of weathering in your area. Look closely at stone buildings, churches, gravestones, brickwork, etc. Build up a record of what you find.

Unit 9
Metamorphic rocks

Metamorphic rocks are formed in a different way to igneous and sedimentary rocks. They are rocks which are changed by heat and pressure. During such changes the rock does not melt.

How heat affects rocks

There are many places within the Earth's crust where rocks come into contact with great heat. If rocks become deeply buried they will be heated. On average, the temperature increases by 30 °C for each kilometre of depth. Metamorphic rocks also form if they are in contact with a direct heat source. The obvious place is near a volcano or an igneous intrusion such as a dyke or sill. Figure 9.1 shows a zone of alteration around a granite bathylith. This is called a **metamorphic aureole**. Heat from the cooling magma has baked the surrounding rocks.

Activity 9.1

What have the original rocks been altered to? Look at Figure 9.1, then copy and complete the following table.

Original rock	Altered rock
Sandstone Shale Mudstone Limestone	

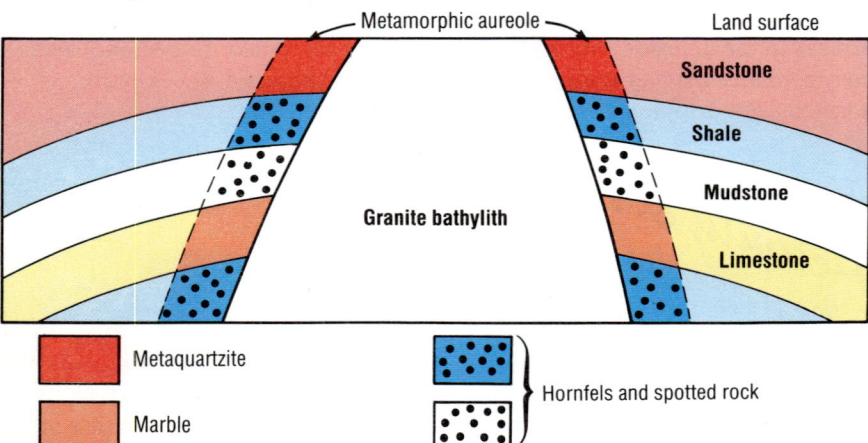

Figure 9.1 A metamorphic aureole around a granite intrusion

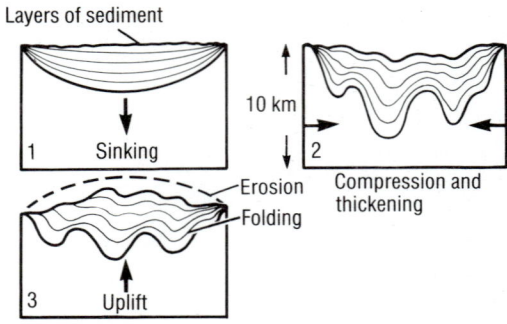

Figure 9.2 Sedimentary layers are squeezed, folded, metamorphosed and uplifted. Try making a model of this with layers of Plasticine

Changes caused by pressure

Within the Earth's crust, there are active zones where there is a lot of movement. This is where rigid sections of the crust called **plates** are moving together and squeezing the rocks caught in between. This creates immense pressure. Rocks buried to a depth of 10 km will be under pressures as high as 20 000 kg per square centimetre. This makes them as soft as putty.

Folding

Rocks are solid, yet capable of flow. This is why many sedimentary layers become folded (Figure 9.2). Fold mountains are formed and uplifted. Compression also causes some layers to become deeply buried. Rocks caught up in this will change because of the great pressure. It is very rare for fossils to survive metamorphism. Usually they are destroyed.

Activity 9.2

Comparing rocks
Examine samples of the rocks mentioned in Activity 9.1 in their pairs. Use a hand lens and a steel point to test for hardness. Write your findings on a record chart.
- What would you say are the main changes to these rocks? Look carefully at the grains. Make sketches to show the main changes.

Activity 9.3

Look at samples of shale, slate, schist, gneiss and granite. Consider the amazing fact that all these rocks are really made of the same materials. The different minerals have formed under different temperatures and pressures.
1. Use a hand lens and a sharp point and test the samples for colour and hardness.
2. Compare the texture of the samples.
3. Use your record chart to write down the main differences between them.
4. Look at a sample of mica. Notice how flaky it is. Compare this to the tiny flakes of mica you can see in the schist.

Activity 9.4

Figure 9.3 Slates at Boscastle, Cornwall

Figure 9.3 shows some slate at Boscastle, Cornwall. You can see clues that tell you about many of the changes this rock has experienced.
1. Make a sketch of this photo.
2. Label small folds, the cleavage layers, small quartz veins, the coin (to show scale).

Summary

How is a metamorphic rock formed? Why do rocks react differently to temperature and pressure? In metamorphism, rocks do not melt – rather they change in response to different temperatures and pressures.

Examples of rocks

At low temperatures but high pressures, mudstones and shales will change to **slate**. The best-quality British slates are found in North Wales. They were formed millions of years ago. This rock is widely used for roofing; it is waterproof and tough but can easily be split into thin sheets. The reason for this is that the clay minerals form new crystal flakes of mica. Because each mica flake is a flat crystal, it turns to face at right angles to the direction of the applied pressure.

At moderate temperatures and high pressures, mudstones and shales will change to **schist**. The mica flakes are bigger and the high pressure causes the mica to grow in parallel bands.

At high temperatures and pressures, mudstones and shales will turn into **gneiss**. Gneiss looks very much like granite. Crystals of quartz, feldspar and mica are present, but unlike granite, the rock has a banded appearance.

Uses of metamorphic materials

Besides slate, there are many other uses for metamorphic rocks and minerals. Marble is used as an ornamental facing stone on buildings. Asbestos is a fibrous mineral that can be powdered, pressed or woven into cloth. It is used to make firemen's suits and is an excellent insulator. Talc is used to make talcum powder and as a lubricant. Diamond is a precious stone which forms under very high pressure. It is used as a gemstone and as a cutting stone because of its extreme hardness.

Questions

1. What are the two main causes of metamorphism? (WP)
2. Explain how the following rocks are changed by heat: sandstone, shale, mudstone, limestone.
3. What is the temperature increase with depth?
4. What is the average temperature and pressure at a depth of 10 km?
5. Explain how slate, schist and gneiss can form from the same original rock.
6. Describe some uses of metamorphic materials.
7. Use a computer program based on the flowchart in Figure 9.4 as a guide to identifying rock samples.

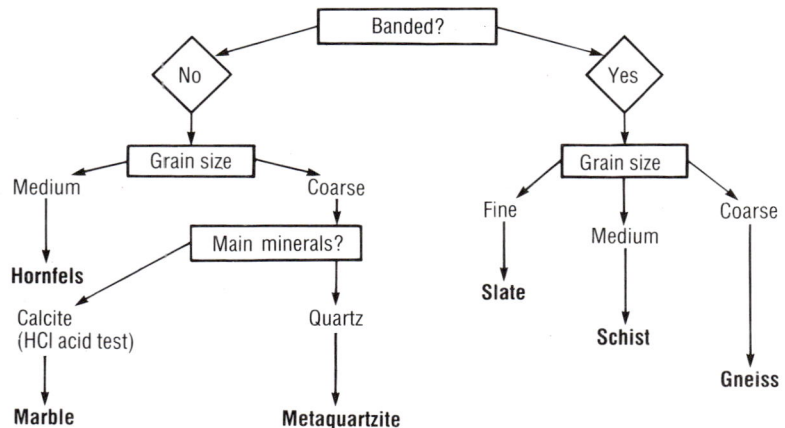

Figure 9.4 This flowchart will help you to identify different rock samples

Unit 10
The rock cycle

Did you know that the three main rock types are linked together in a great cycle of change? Did you know that new rocks form as older rocks are destroyed (see Figure 10.1)?

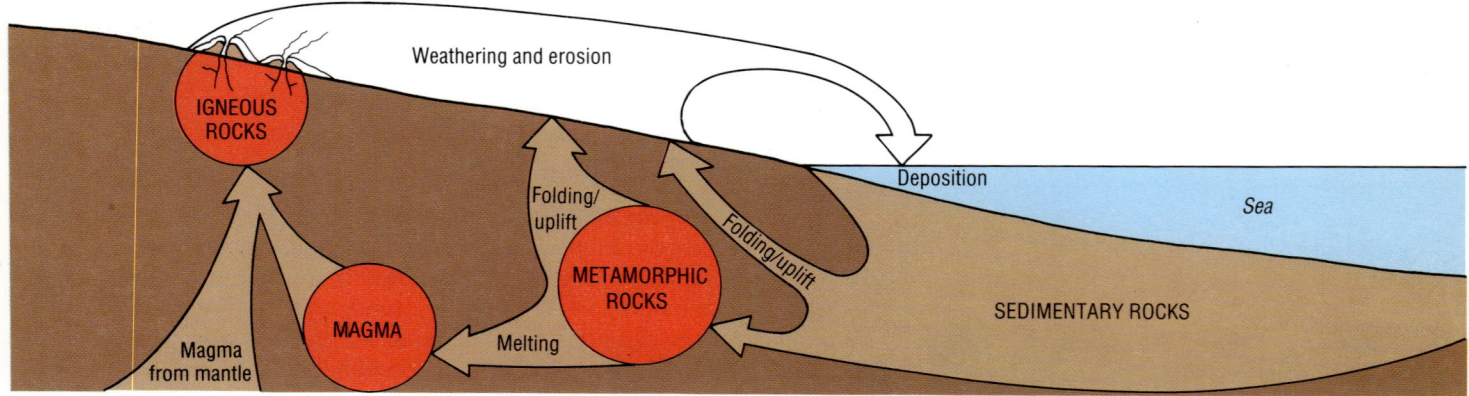

Figure 10.1 The rock cycle

Volcanoes erode away to become layers of sediment. These in turn may be folded and uplifted to become land, or deeply buried to become metamorphic rocks. Deeply buried sediments may re-melt to become magma. This in turn will produce new rock in volcanoes and intrusions. The whole cycle will then begin again. The complete cycle takes millions of years.

Weathering and erosion

The forces of weathering and erosion slowly wear away volcanoes. Igneous intrusions are exposed at the surface as the rocks covering them are removed. Minerals like quartz that are found in many igneous rocks end up as sand. Igneous rocks like basalt and granite eventually become broken fragments of sand, mud and silt.

Erosion can involve the movement of rock grains in a number of different ways: by gravity down a slope, by streams and rivers, by ice, by wind, by sea waves and tides.

Gravity and rivers

Gravity is directly responsible for the movement of weathered rock fragments down hillsides, as in avalanches, landslides and mudflows. Many slopes have piles of loose boulders at the foot of them, known as scree (Figure 10.2). Gravity can also cause the slow movement of soil downslope. This is known as soil creep.

Rivers carry huge amounts of sediment to the sea. The movement of loose sand and pebbles can itself cause more erosion. For example, the pebbles carried by the river cut a deeper and wider channel for the water. Eventually a V-shaped valley is formed. At the mouth of a river the sediment is dropped to form new layers of sediment. What are the names given to sand and mud once they are compacted and cemented as sedimentary rock?

Activity 10.1

Discuss the following:
1 What are the main effects of gravity on erosion?
2 Why do rivers flow towards the sea?
3 What gives rivers the energy they need to erode their river valleys?

Figure 10.2 These screes at Wastwater were formed by the effects of gravity

Figure 10.3 A rock pedestal – this has been formed by wind action

Activity 10.2

Consider what can happen to a layer of mud, as it passes through the rock cycle:

mud → shale → slate → schist → gneiss → granite

Draw this sequence as a cycle diagram. On your diagram label the 'igneous', 'sedimentary' and 'metamorphic' stages. **WP**

Figure 10.4 An eroded volcanic plug, Le Puy, France

Ice and wind

In cold climates, ice sheets and glaciers have rocks embedded on their undersides. As they move, they scrape over the land like huge sheets of sand paper and remove vast amounts of rock fragments. All this material will eventually form new sedimentary rock.

In dry climates, wind will pick up dust and sand. When the sand is blown against bare rocks it can wear away the softer layers, especially those near to the ground (see Figure 10.3).

Wave action and deposition

Waves will pick up pebbles and hurl them against the foot of a cliff, breaking off more rock fragments. Tides and currents will move this material away to be deposited elsewhere.

When all the rock fragments come to rest they form layers of sediment. The sea-floor is where most of the new sedimentary rock layers form. In time, the lower layers harden as they are compacted beneath the weight of newer layers.

Downwarping and compression

The sheer weight of sediments on the sea-floor can make the Earth's crust sag downwards. This allows even more sediment to collect.

Eventually the layers may be folded as they come under sideways pressure. If they are buried deep enough, some rocks will be changed by heat and pressure to become metamorphic rocks.

Uplift and re-melting

Pressures deep within the Earth can cause buried rocks to be uplifted as land again. Mount Everest is made of folds of sedimentary rocks with sea-shells that were once on the sea-floor.

Some sedimentary rocks encounter so much heat that they re-melt; in other words, they become magma and will cool to form igneous rocks again.

The time factor

The cycle of rock change is a very slow one. Figure 10.4 shows the plug of an old eroded volcano that can still be seen after 300 million years. It takes even longer for the fragments from the volcano to settle on the sea-floor and become rock again. In time the same sediments could re-melt to become part of a new volcano – but this would take many millions of years.

Summary

The rock cycle is a relationship between the processes of rock formation and erosion. Weathering and erosion act to break down surface rocks and form new sedimentary layers. Underground processes turn soft sediment into new metamorphic and igneous rocks. Then the long cycle begins again.

Questions

1. Are the following statements **true** or **false**?
   a. Erosion is the process that wears away rocks.
   b. Only soft rocks are worn away.
   c. All erosion involves movement of rock material.
2. Describe what would happen to one quartz crystal from a granite intrusion as it passes through the rock cycle. **WP**

Unit 11
Earth structure

How can something going on thousands of kilometres beneath our feet protect us from harmful rays from space? What is this force 'shield'? What has it got to do with the structure of the Earth? What is the Earth like inside?

Although no-one has ever been to the Earth's centre, we do know something of its structure (see Figure 11.1).

The inner and outer cores

Right at the centre of the Earth is a ball of very hot and dense material of radius 1221 km. It is metallic and is made of iron and nickel. The temperature is over 3000 °C, yet the ball does not melt. It stays solid because of the extremely high pressures. The pressure at the Earth's centre is 3 million times of that at the surface.

The outer core is made of the same material as the inner core, but it exists in a liquid state. This is because it is under less pressure. The temperature of this layer is about the same. Its thickness is 2250 km.

The mantle

The mantle is made of solid rock. The pressure is high enough to stop the rocks melting, even though they are at very high temperatures. The upper layers of the mantle are thought to flow slowly (rather like the way solid Plasticine can flow). The movement is caused by **convection**. Hot rocks move very slowly towards the surface, sometimes melting the lower crust to produce volcanoes. The slowly rising rock cools as it loses heat through the crust. Then it moves sideways and eventually sinks.

The crust

The crust is a very thin layer of surface rock. On average, it is between 8 and 35 km thick (see Figure 11.2). There are two kinds of crust:
(a) older, thicker continental crust,
(b) younger, thinner oceanic crust.
Continental crust is made of many different kinds of rock which have often been folded by earth movements. Oceanic crust is mainly made of a rock called basalt. It is formed by volcanic activity on the ocean floor.

Density

The layers that make up the Earth do not have the same density. Density is a measurement of the mass in grams (g), packed into each cubic centimetre (cm^3). The whole Earth has a density of 5.5 g/cm^3. At the surface, the oceans have a density of 1 g/cm^3, and the crust 2.8 g/cm^3. This means that layers deep within the Earth are much denser. The core is thought to have a density of over 10 g/cm^3. The crust is light and 'floats' on the mantle below it.

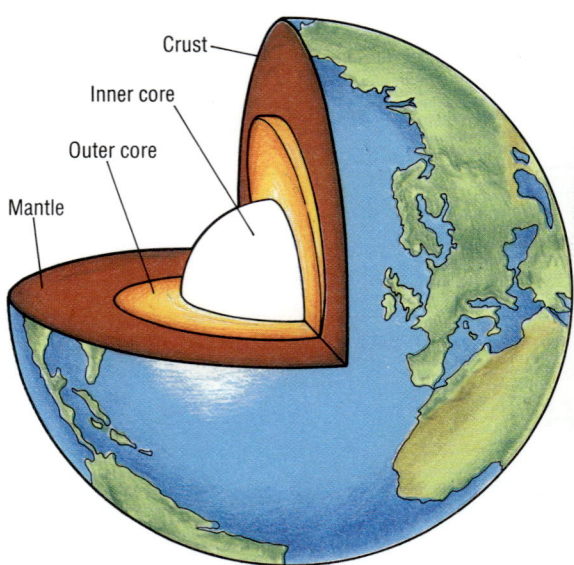

Figure 11.1 The Earth's structure

Activity 11.1

How convection works
Fill a beaker with water. Then without disturbing the water, drop a few potassium permanganate crystals down a glass tube so that they rest on the bottom of the beaker. Gently heat the beaker.
1. What happens directly above the pile of crystals?
2. Why does this happen?
3. What is the direction of flow of the cooler water in the beaker?
4. Make a sketch of the apparatus you have used and write down your results.

Activity 11.2

1. Add together all the thickness figures for the different layers. How far is it from the surface to the centre of the Earth?
2. Using graph paper, draw a scaled line to show the thickness of the Earth. On your line mark off the boundaries between each layer. Your diagram could look like that in Figure 11.3.

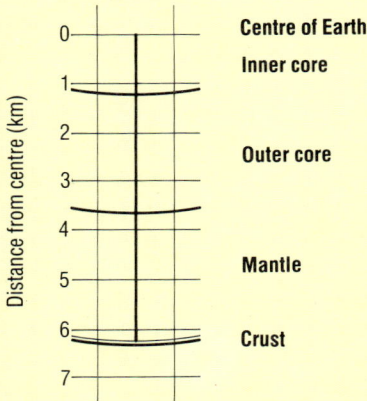

Figure 11.3 Drawing the depth of the Earth's layers to scale

Activity 11.4

Making a magnetic model of the Earth

Put a piece of magnetic magnetite inside a ball of Plasticine. Place the model 'Earth' under a piece of paper and sprinkle iron filings on the paper.

1. What patterns do you see?
2. Do the lines of force look like the pattern of the real Earth's magnetic field (see Figure 11.4)?

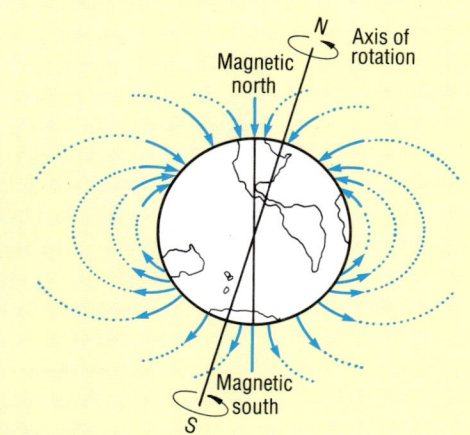

Figure 11.4 The Earth's magnetic field

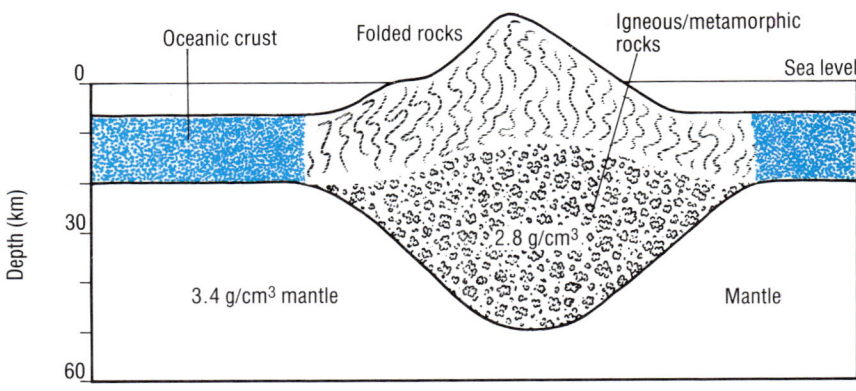

Figure 11.2 Continental and oceanic crust

Activity 11.3

The Earth's magnetism

Work in groups.
Suspend a bar magnet by a piece of cotton. Allow it to rotate freely. Make sure you do this well away from any metals that might attract the magnet, such as steel table legs. Does your bar magnet line up in the same position as the magnets of other groups? Use a magnetic compass to check the North–South direction in your room. Does this match up with the position of the suspended bar magnet? The compass needle is a small bar magnet and it lines itself up, North–South, in the magnetic influence of the Earth. This is known as the Earth's **magnetic field**.

How magnetism protects us

The Earth's magnetic field acts as a natural 'shield' and protects us from harmful **cosmic rays**. These are charged particles that travel through space from the Sun. The circulation of liquids in the outer core is the cause of the Earth's magnetism making the Earth behave like a giant bar magnet.

Summary

The Earth is made of layers of rock. Deep inside the Earth is the origin of the magnetic field that protects the planet from much of the harmful rays from the Sun. What do we know about this internal structure? How thick is each layer?

Questions

1. How does the outer core 'shield' the Earth?
2. How does convection occur in the mantle?
3. Write notes explaining the Earth's magnetism.
4. What is meant by density? Explain how the Earth varies in density.

Unit 12
Where earthquakes happen

Is it true that there are never any big earthquakes in Britain? Where do you have to be to experience a really big earthquake?

Figure 12.1 shows where most of the world's earthquakes happen. Notice how the pattern of epicentres is in long narrow curving belts. Outside these zones earthquakes are rare but they still sometimes happen. For example, in 1984 there was an earthquake measuring 5.5 on the Richter scale at Porthmadog in North Wales. However, the great depth of the **focus** (point of origin) of the earthquake meant that there was little surface damage.

> **Activity 12.1**
>
> Slowly bend a pencil or thin piece of wood until it snaps. Note how all the stored energy is suddenly released.

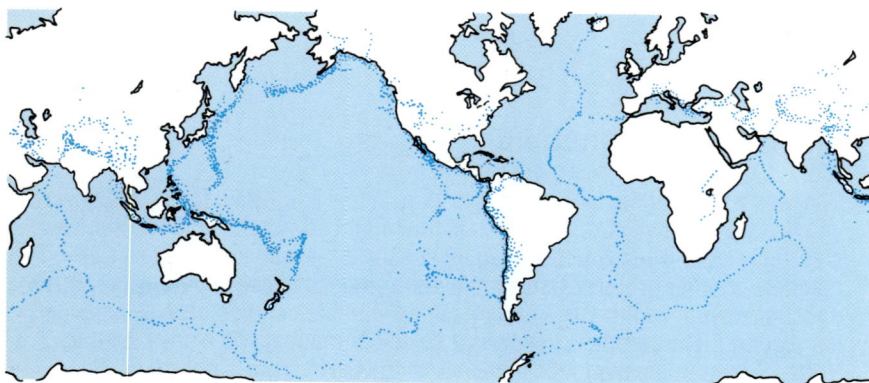

Figure 12.1 The distribution of the main earthquake epicentres. Where would the San Francisco earthquake be on this map? (Each dot is an earthquake)

Plates

The outer surface of the Earth is split into large rigid sections called **plates**. Figure 12.2 shows the world's plates. Compare it to Figure 12.1. What do you notice about the way the two maps match up? Each plate is a large rigid section of crust and upper mantle rock, about 100 km thick. The plates are moving against each other and these movements produce earthquakes at their edges where they are in contact with each other. The most severe

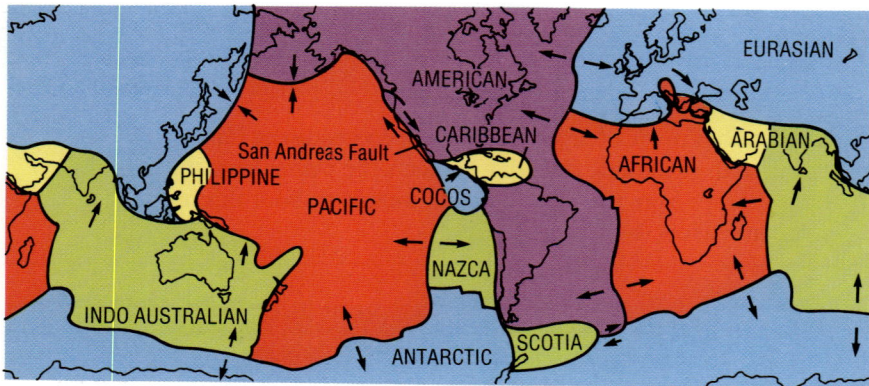

Figure 12.2 The Earth's plates and their main directions of movement. The black lines are plate boundaries

Figure 12.3 The San Andreas fault

Safer buildings for a shaky future

Many people died in the San Francisco earthquake because the upper section of a road bridge collapsed, crushing cars on the lower section. Other people died in buildings that could not stand up to the vibrations. The buildings collapsed and people were crushed. Most of the newer Californian buildings have special foundations resistant to earthquakes. The 48-storey Transamerica Pyramid in San Francisco sits on a 7 m thick concrete mat. This acts like an anchor and makes the building bottom-heavy to resist overturning in an earthquake. New high-rise buildings are supported on piles driven 50 m into the ground. They are built with steel framing.

Activity 12.2

Imagine you are a reporter. Design a front page spread with stories about a major earthquake and the efforts of scientists to forecast it. **DTP**

Summary

Earthquakes are a great threat to human life and property – but where do earthquakes occur and why do they happen? Earthquakes are caused by a sudden release of stored energy in underground rocks.

Questions

1 The Earth's surface is made up of seven main plates with lots of smaller ones. The largest plate is the Pacific plate. List the other six main plates.
2 Name two main plates with no continental land area.
3 Of which plate are the British Isles a part?
4 What is the thickness of a plate?
5 Explain why movement along a transform fault only happens at intervals.

earthquakes happen along huge cracks called **transform faults**. Over many years pressure is stored in the rocks on either side of the fault. The fault surface is often rough, so there is no movement. Hence, the pressure continues to build. An earthquake happens when, all of a sudden, the roughness and friction of the rocks is overcome. Then there is a sudden jerky movement which releases the built-up pressure and causes the earthquake.

The San Andreas Fault in California, USA, stretches for 950 km along the West coast (Figure 12.3). Unfortunately large cities like Los Angeles and San Francisco lie very close to this fault. In 1989, San Francisco was hit by an earthquake, measuring 6.9 on the Richter scale, and 272 people were killed. The usual movement along the fault is about 5 cm per year, but for over 80 years there had been no movement in this area of the fault. If all the possible stored energy had been released in one earthquake, how much would the fault have moved? Fortunately for San Francisco this was not 'the big one'. Badly-built houses and bridges fell down, but many of the purpose-built earthquake-resistant buildings survived intact.

Measuring the strain across the fault

There is little doubt that an even bigger disaster will happen soon, when there is larger movement along the San Andreas fault. Figure 12.4 shows some of the ways that scientists are measuring strain across the fault.

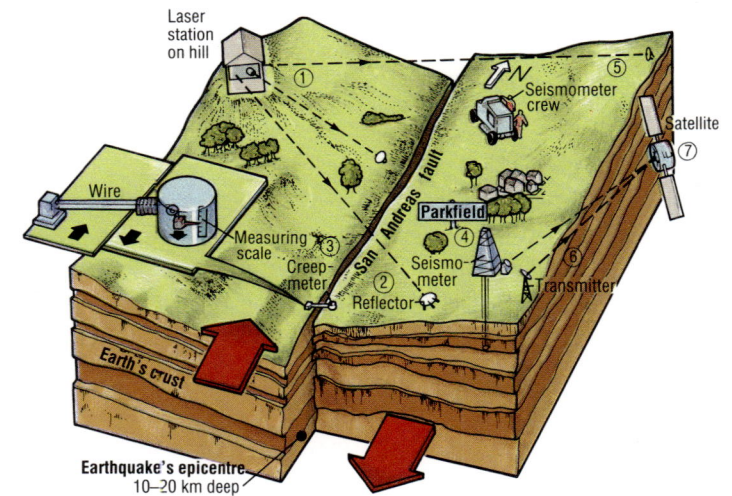

Figure 12.4 Measuring the strain across the San Andreas fault line. 1 Laser beams track tiny movements bouncing beams off reflectors 2. 3 Creepmeters measure displacement on wires stretched across the fault. 4 Seismometers in boreholes measure small changes in water levels. 5 Surface seismometers. 6 Electronic data transmitted to 7 satellite, for processing back in the laboratory

Laser beams are bounced off reflectors. Any change in the length of the beam will show some movement has taken place. Seismometers are used in boreholes nearby to detect tiny vibrations. The creepmeter measures the slightest strain in the rocks.

- Look at Figure 12.4 and explain how the creepmeter works.

The readings from all these instruments are transmitted to the laboratory many miles away, using the satellite. Scientists hope that if they can measure the build up of strain either side of the fault, then they will be able to warn people of a possible earthquake. This could save many lives.

Unit 13
Uses of earthquake shockwaves

Earthquakes are dangerous – they cause untold human misery, death and destruction of property. So how can they be useful?

Evidence for the Earth's structure

It is unlikely that people will ever travel to the centre of the Earth and find out what it is like by direct methods. The pressures and temperatures would be far too great. However, it is possible to learn a great deal about the Earth's structure by using indirect methods. This is where shockwaves created by earthquakes have proved so useful. They can be used rather like X-rays, to detect what the Earth is like inside.

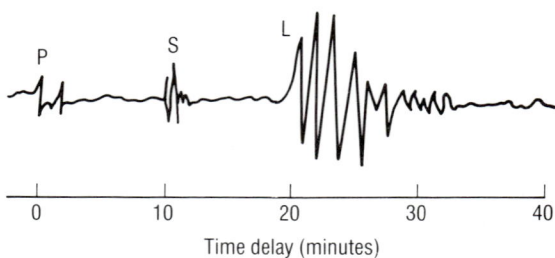

Figure 13.1 A seismograph recording

Seismographs

Figure 13.1 shows the record of one earthquake made by a seismograph. The vibrations of the shockwaves show three pulses, caused by three kinds of shockwave, known as P, S and L waves.

How shockwaves travel

(You can find out more about these waves if you read *Earth, Atmosphere and Space*, Book 2.) The shockwaves are all produced from the same earthquake at the same time, but they travel at different velocities. This is because they pass through the rocks in different ways.

P waves
P waves are compressional waves. The rock material is first compressed and then stretched. Therefore the motion of each particle of rock is backwards and forwards. Imagine a line of cars where the last car crashes into the one just in front. The shock is transferred through the line in a shunt accident. This is how P waves travel. The shock passes through most rocks at about 8 km/s.

S waves
S waves are transverse or shear waves. Their crests and troughs rise and fall at right angles to the direction of travel of the wavefront. They can only travel through rigid materials at about half the speed of P waves. They cannot pass through liquids.

L waves
L waves are the slowest of all. They can only travel through the surface rocks of the Earth's crust. These waves have a rolling motion and cause the greatest destruction in an earthquake.

Activity 13.1

Look at Figure 13.1.
1 Which kind of shockwave is the first to be recorded and therefore travels fastest?
2 Which is the slowest shockwave?
3 What is the time interval between the P and S wave, and the S and L wave?

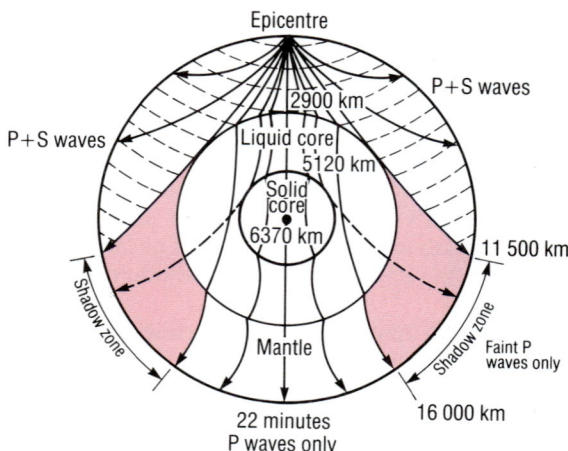

Figure 13.2 How P and S waves travel through the Earth

Activity 13.2

Refraction

You can make a model of this by placing a beaker filled with water in the centre of a round piece of white card (Figure 13.3). Then shine a torch at the side of the beaker. How does the beaker focus the light? Can you see a shadow zone? How does this model compare with the real effect of shockwaves bending as they pass through the core?

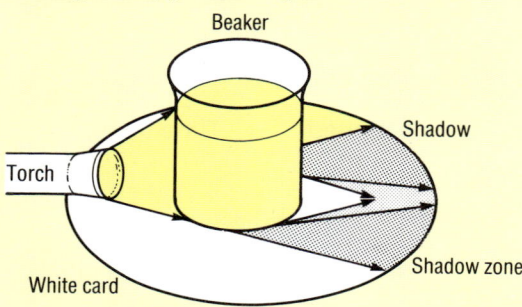

Figure 13.3 A model to show refraction

Answer the following questions (discuss then write).
- How do we know that there is a core? **WP**
- How do we know that all or part of the core is a liquid?
- In addition to the evidence from shockwaves, what other clues are there to the fact that the Earth must be much denser inside? (To answer this, you may need to look up the section on 'Density' in Unit 11)

Using seismic waves to 'see' the Earth's core

P and S waves can be used to 'X-ray' deep inside the Earth. When a big earthquake happens, enough energy is released to make the whole planet shudder slightly. P and S waves travel out in all directions, through the body of the Earth. As they go deeper, they travel through denser rocks and begin to curve out towards the surface again. If the Earth were made of the same material throughout, then you would expect to see an even web pattern. In fact, what actually happens is that no S waves can pass through the centre of the Earth. Something stops them and absorbs them. Figure 13.2 shows this in more detail. The evidence for the core comes from the way that P and S waves behave. The zone where P and S waves are absent or rare is known as the **shadow zone**. This zone is created by the bending inwards of P waves as they enter the core. This is known as **refraction**. This is evidence that the core is much denser than the mantle. The same bending effect can be seen when light rays pass from less-dense air to denser water.

What is the evidence for a solid inner core?

Very faint P waves appearing inside the shadow zone show that there is a smaller inner solid core, which bounces the P waves outwards.

How thick is each layer?

Figure 13.4 shows how the depth of the core–mantle boundary is known. Notice how P and S waves pick up speed as they travel through the mantle, to a depth of about 2900 km. Then P waves suddenly slow down and S waves disappear altogether as they enter the core.

Summary

Even hazards like earthquakes have their uses. Their shockwaves can be used to X-ray the inner layers of the Earth. A close study of seismic waves reveals a liquid outer core and a solid dense inner core.

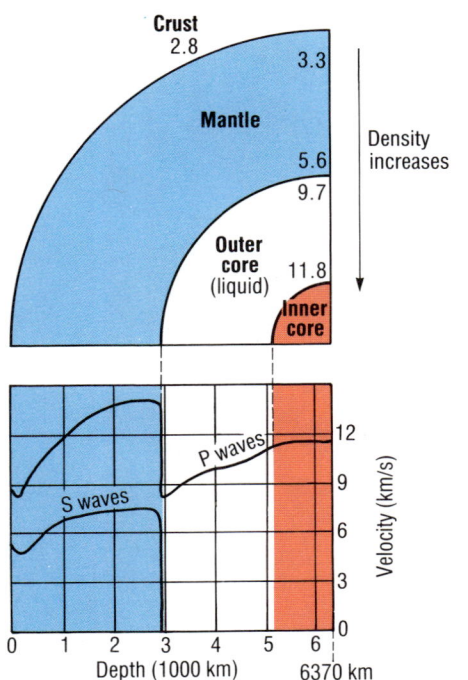

Figure 13.4 How wave velocity relates to Earth layer

Questions

1. Why is a study of shockwaves of such value?
2. A delay of 1 minute between P and S waves on a seismogram would mean the earthquake was 1000 km away. The seismogram in Figure 13.1 shows a delay of 10 minutes. How far away was this earthquake? **WP**
3. Compare the different ways in which shockwaves travel. If possible also refer to *Earth, Atmosphere and Space*, Book 2.
4. Which shockwave cannot travel through liquid? Which causes the most surface damage?
5. What causes the shadow zone? What does this tell us about the Earth's structure?
6. How do we know that the inner core is solid?
7. Explain what the evidence is for the Earth's structure, as shown in Figure 13.4. **WP**

Unit 14
Earth movements

Did you know that all the land in the world was once one huge continent called **Pangaea**? This was 200 million years ago. Then it slowly broke up and the separate parts became the continents we know today (Figure 14.1).

The theory that the continents slowly move is known as the theory of **continental drift**. This theory is not particularly new. Before World War I, an American called Frank Taylor and a German called Alfred Wegener, both working independently, published theories that said the continents either side of the Atlantic Ocean had once been joined together. The idea that continents actually move may seem surprising. Many people at the time did not think very much of the theory and it was rejected as a wild idea. It is now much more widely accepted because of the evidence provided by plate movements. Careful measurements also show that the continents, together with their plates, are still moving about 5 cm every year – as fast as your fingernails grow. This may not sound very fast, but it is in terms of Earth history. One million years is a short time in the Earth's history – in that time a continent could move by 50 km.

Activity 14.1

Rates of continental drift
Copy and complete the following table.

Distance moved	Time taken
5 cm	1 year
50 cm	10 years
100 cm (1 m)	? years
? m	100 years
10 m	200 years
100 m	? years
1000 m (1 km)	20 000 years

What is the evidence?

Matching coastlines and rock structures
The idea that the continents were once joined together comes from matching up the shape of facing coastlines. Look at Figure 14.2. You will see how well Africa and South America fit along the coastlines which now face each other across the Atlantic Ocean. Also within each continent there are very old rock structures called **shields**, with folded rocks in between them. These rock structures also match up.

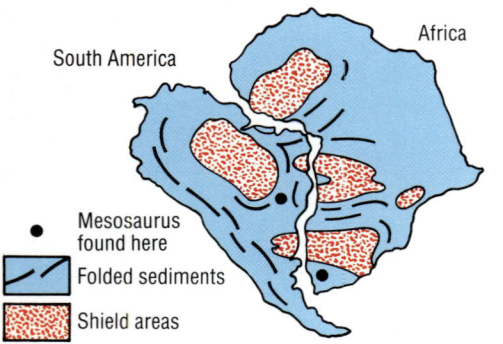

Figure 14.2 South America and Africa once were one huge continent

Fossil evidence
Fossils of the reptile Mesosaurus and fossil leaves of a fern tree have been found in both continents. In each case the fossil comes from rocks of the same type and age – yet the continents are now 6000 km apart. These animals and plants lived before the two continents began the process of continental drift. The space between the two continents has been filled by the 'new' Atlantic Ocean and a 'new' seabed which has formed mainly from volcanic lava.

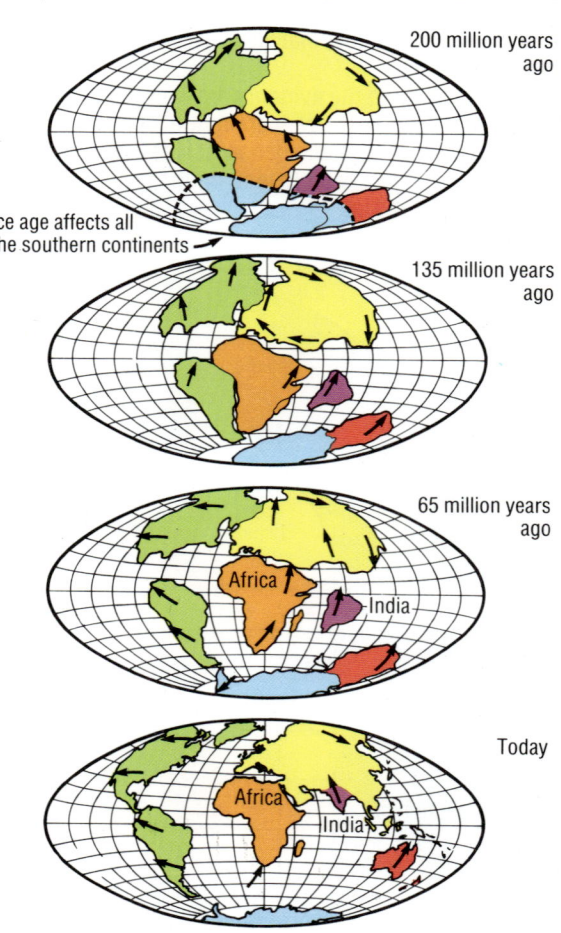

Figure 14.1 Continental drift

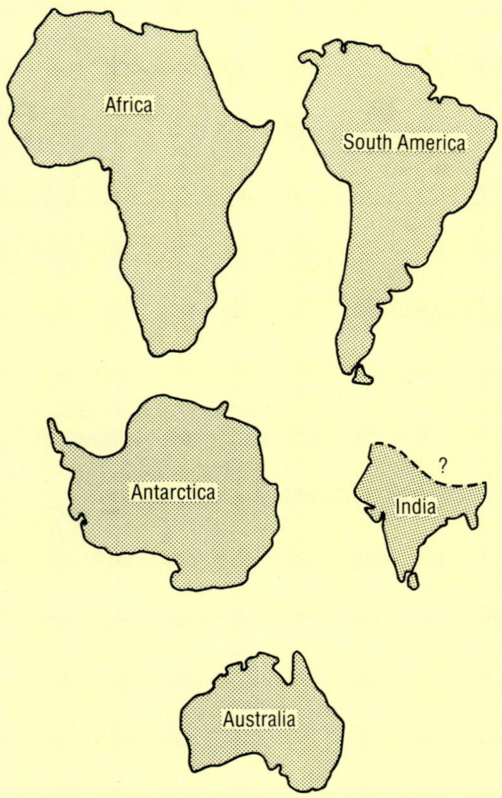

Activity 14.2 Putting part of Pangaea together again

Discuss and work in pairs.
Trace the shapes of the southern continents in Figure 14.3 onto card. Cut out the shapes and try to find the best way of fitting them together. How do your efforts compare with the map in Figure 14.1 and with the work of other pairs?

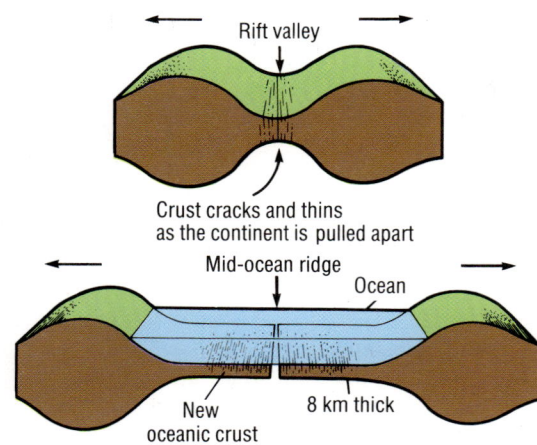

Figure 14.3 The southern continents. Do they fit together?

Continental drift and rift valleys

When two landmasses drift away from each other, the crust between them gets thinner. Long tension cracks called **faults** form as the rocks are pulled apart. The ground between the faults often sinks to form wide **rift valleys**. Molten rock called magma squeezes its way along the faults and volcanoes form at the surface. As the rift widens, it is flooded by the sea. As the continents drift apart, the narrow sea becomes a wide ocean (Figure 14.4). Today the Atlantic Ocean is still widening. Since Christopher Columbus sailed to America, the Atlantic has widened by about 15 m.

Mid-ocean ridges

The Atlantic Ocean is an example of an opening ocean because the Americas are moving away from Europe and Africa. You will see from Figure 14.4 that the seabed is made of new rock. This is lava from submarine volcanoes. It forms a layer called **oceanic crust** which is about 8 km thick. In the middle of the Atlantic there is a ridge. Ocean ridges form the longest and largest 'mountains' in the world. They are not noticed very much because they are mostly below sea level. On the top of the ridge there is a rift valley and a lot of volcanic activity. This is where new oceanic crust forms. This then spreads out sideways, pushing the continents apart. Look at the world maps in Unit 12 – Figures 12.1 and 12.2 on page 26.

Figure 14.4 New crust forms as the continents separate and the sea becomes a wide ocean

Summary

The continents are moving slowly across the Earth's surface. Why is this happening and what is the evidence for it? These movements have produced other features such as rift valleys, widening oceans, ocean ridges and new oceanic crust.

Activity 14.3

- What marks the position of the mid-Atlantic ridge in Figures 12.1 and 12.2?

Questions

1. How many kilometres per year do the continents drift?
2. How many years ago did South America split away from Africa? (Note: there is now a gap of about 5000 km between the continents and they have moved apart at a rate of 50 km every 1 million years.)
3. What is a 'shield' area?
4. Complete the following sentences using the bracketed words below.

   The oceanic crust is .... km thick. The ...... crust is much thicker. The ...... rocks are found in the continents, whereas the ...... crust is much younger.

   (oldest, 8, continental, oceanic)
5. Summarise the evidence that supports the theory of continental drift.
6. The Atlantic is described as an 'opening' ocean. What does this mean? When did the ocean begin to open?

Unit 15
Fold and block mountains

Did you know that the world's highest mountain, from base to summit, is a volcano? Mauna Loa, Hawaii rises 10 203 m from the seabed, of which 4205 m is the island above sea level.

Did you know that the Himalayan range is the world's biggest mountain range? Ninety six of the world's 109 highest peaks are found there.

The highest point in the world is Mount Everest. Its summit is 8840 m above sea level. The rock layers near the summit are made of folded sediments. They have been uplifted from the seabed and have fossilised sea-shells in them.

How fold mountains form

Sideways pressure on rock layers produces folds. Upfolds are called **anticlines** and downfolds are called **synclines**. Sometimes the pressure is so great that much larger folds called **nappes** are formed. The top part of a fold may slide over the bottom part along a **thrust** fault (Figure 15.1). The sideways pressure for the formation of fold mountains is caused by the collision of two or more of the world's plates. Mount Everest is in the Himalayan range. The whole mountain range is made of rock layers that have been folded and crumpled in the last 30 million years as the Indian plate collided with the Asian plate (Figure 15.2).

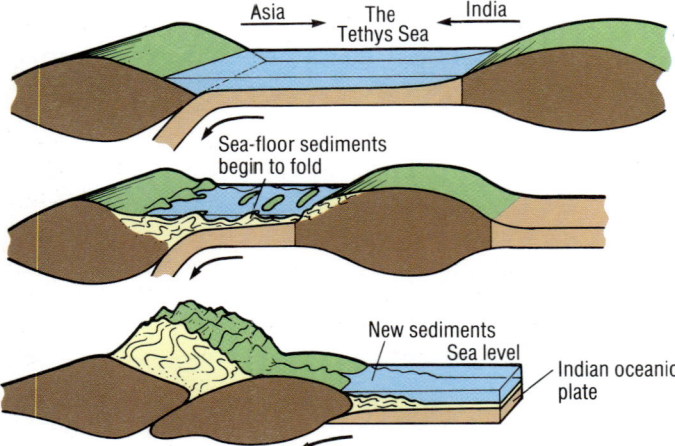

Figure 15.2 How the Himalayan mountains were formed. The Asian and Indian plates collide. The Tethys Ocean (sea) gets smaller and the layers of sediment get squeezed up into folds. Erosion has carved them into mountain peaks

How the Himalayan mountains were formed

The Asian and Indian plates collided as shown in Figure 15.2. The Tethys Sea became smaller and the layers of sediment were squeezed up into folds. Erosion carved them into mountain peaks. As the Indian plate moved northwards, sediments on the floor of the Tethys Sea were compressed into

Activity 15.1

Work in pairs.
How high are Mauna Loa and Mount Everest in kilometres? Make a scaled graph to show the relative heights of the two mountains. Discuss then write about the following questions. **WP**

1. How do you know that the rocks on Mount Everest used to be in the sea?
2. How could the layers of sea-floor sediment have become uplifted?

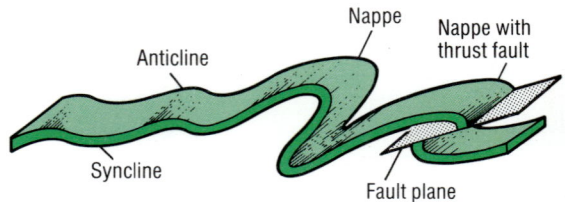

Figure 15.1 How a layer of sediment folds

Activity 15.2

Work in pairs. Discuss and then write about the following questions.
1. Do you think there would be any earthquakes in the Himalayas? Give reasons for your answer.
2. The world map (Figure 15.3) shows the world's main fold mountains.
   a. What do the arrows stand for?
   b. Compare this map to the map showing the world's plates on page 26. Are there any similarities?
   c. Make a copy of Figure 15.3 using an outline map of the world. Use an atlas to look up the names of the mountain ranges marked by letters. Label them on your map.
3. What is the nearest fold mountain range to Britain? Which two plates collided to form this range?

Activity 15.3

Making fold mountains
Press a layer of Plasticine about 1 cm thick onto a flat, flexible baking knife. Slide the blade underneath a clamped chopping board. In this model the chopping board is like the Asian continent and the knife is like the sinking front edge of the plate.
1. What happens to the Plasticine?
2. Why doesn't the Plasticine slide under with the blade? Why do layers of sediments fold instead of sinking with the plate?

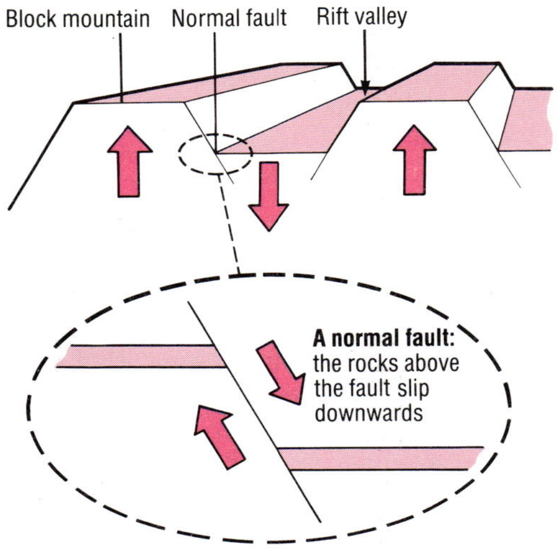

folds. The thinner front edge of the Indian plate sank beneath the thicker Asian continent and the sediments were scraped off into folds. Today the Indian plate is still pushing northwards at a rate of 4 cm per year. The mountains are still being lifted upwards even though erosion by ice, streams and rivers removes millions of tonnes of rock material every year. The low-density continental masses behave rather like two giant corks, floating on the plastic mantle. The Indian continent cannot sink with the rest of the Indian plate back into the mantle. This means that there is, in effect, a double thickness of continental crust beneath the Himalayan mountains.

The world's fold mountains

The fold mountain 'chains' are in long narrow belts. They are found at active plate boundaries where plates are in collision. Earthquakes and volcanoes are also found along the same belts.

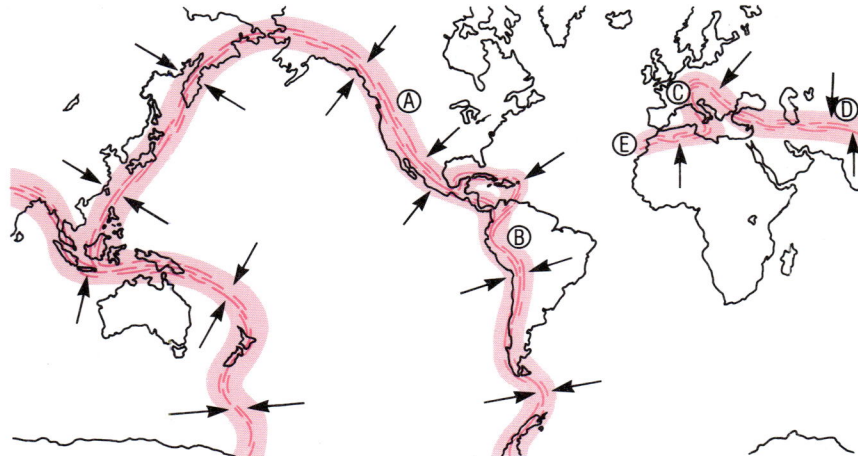

Figure 15.3 The world's fold mountains. The fold mountain 'chains' are in long narrow belts. They are found at active plate boundaries where plates are in collision

Block mountains

Plate movements not only compress rocks into folds. When two plates are moving away from each other, tensional forces stretch the rocks of the crust and pull them apart. Eventually the rocks may break and move along faults. When a wedge of land sinks between **normal faults**, a rift valley forms (Figure 15.4). This takes up some of the tension. One good example is the rift valley in East Africa. Block mountains or **horsts** are formed when blocks of land slip upwards between faults. The block mountains of the Ruwenzori near the East African rift have formed in this way. Block mountains and rift valleys are also linked to plate movements, but unlike fold mountains, they are caused by tension, not compression.

The Midland Valley of Scotland between the Highland Boundary fault and the Southern Uplands fault is one British example of a rift valley. Look this up on a map of the geology of the British Isles. How wide is the valley?

Figure 15.4 Block mountains and rift valleys. The arrows show the direction of movement

Questions

1. What are the differences between anticlines, synclines and nappes?
2. Two different kinds of fault are mentioned in this unit.
   a. What are they called?
   b. Which kind of fault forms because of tension (pulling apart) and which forms because of compression (pushing together)?
3. What were the two plates that collided to form the Himalayas?
4. Where did the folded sediments come from?
5. Why are the Himalayas higher than any other mountain range? (Discuss the answer.)

Summary
The mountain ranges of the world are mostly made of uplifted sea-floor sediments. How did they form? What are block mountains? Fold and block mountains are clear evidence of the continual movements of the Earth's surface rocks.

Unit 16
Plate tectonics

Why do the continents move? What are plates? If continents move apart, what happens to fill the space between them?

The two kinds of crust

The landmasses of the Earth are made of low-density, thick continental crust. The rocks are often very old. 3800 million years is the age of the oldest rock found so far. On the other hand, samples of rock taken from the ocean floor show that oceanic crust is denser and much newer. Nowhere is it older than 200 million years. It is also quite thin and mainly made of basalt. Studies show that the rocks on the floors of large oceans like the Atlantic have formed between the continents as they have drifted apart. In the case of the Atlantic Ocean, as North and South America separated from Europe and Africa, volcanoes along the line of the mid-ocean ridge produced new rocks. This new crust is still being created and added along the mid-ocean ridges today (Figure 16.1).

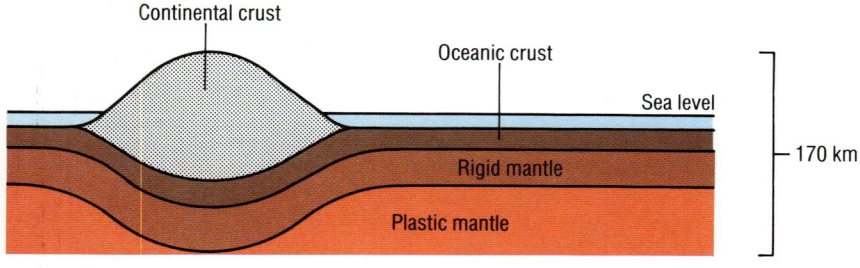

Figure 16.1 The relative thicknesses of continental and oceanic plates

What does 'tectonics' mean?

When you have completed Activity 16.1 you will realise that the edges of plates are active zones where there are many earthquakes, volcanoes, faults and folds. These features are produced by **tectonic** processes. In the centres of plates there is far less disturbance and these features are much rarer. In effect, the plates are jostling for position and the resulting movements cause most of the changes along their edges.

How do plates move?

Plates move quite slowly – no more than about 6 cm a year. It is thought that they move in response to heat flow inside the Earth. Rocks in the mantle behave rather like Plasticine. They are solid, yet able to flow very slowly. There is an upward movement of hot plastic rocks in the mantle, as shown in Figure 16.2. At the surface the rocks spread sideways, where they cool and eventually sink again. The sideways movement drags along the plate above it as well.

Activity 16.1

Look carefully at the map of the world's plates, Figure 12.2 on page 26. The Pacific plate has the largest area.
1. Use an atlas to help you find Iceland. Write down the names of the two plates that make up the island.
2. Compare Figure 12.2 with the map of the world's earthquakes (Figure 12.1) – how do the two maps match up?
3. Now compare the map with the map showing the location of the world's fold mountains (Figure 15.3) – how do the two maps match up?

What is plate tectonics?

The theory of plate tectonics suggests that the Earth's surface is divided into a number of segments, known as plates. These are shown in Figure 12.2, page 26. Each plate is a rigid slab of rock. Plates are about 70 km thick under the oceans and up to 150 km thick under the continents. They are made of thinner oceanic or thicker continental crust, together with the top part of the mantle.

Activity 16.2

Discuss then write.
1. Why does hot material rise toward the surface?
2. Why do upper mantle rocks sink as they cool?
Look back at Activity 11.1 to give you some ideas.

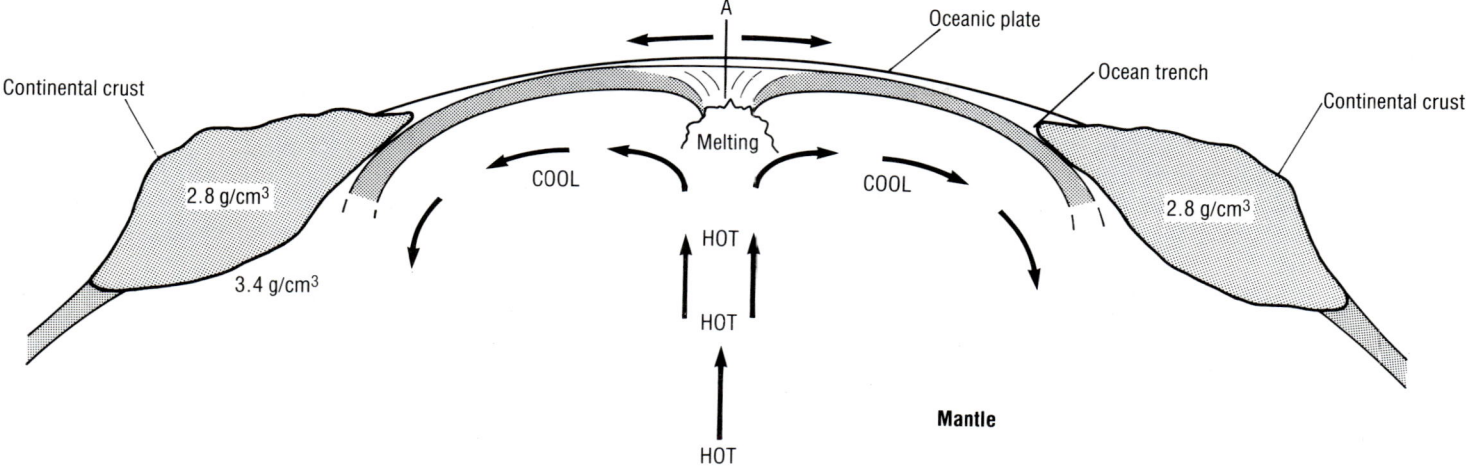

Figure 16.2 The effect of convection currents

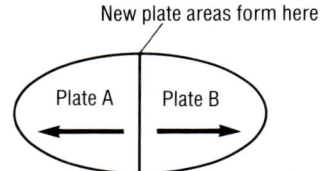

(a) Plates moving apart (constructive margin). The rocks are stretched by tensional forces

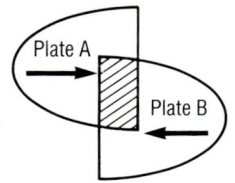

(b) Plates in collision (destructive margin). One plate slides beneath the other. The rocks are buckled by compression

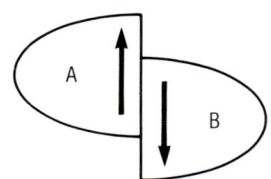

(c) Plates sliding past each other (conservative margin). The plates build up stress along transform faults. Sudden movements release this pent-up energy, causing earthquakes

Figure 16.3 The three main kinds of plate margin

Activity 16.3

The effect of convection
Set up the experiment in Activity 11.1.

1. What happens to warm water at the bottom of the beaker?
2. In which direction does cold water from the top of the beaker move?
3. Float a piece of paper on the water surface. Explain what happens to the paper.
4. Make a sketch of this activity and fully describe the process. In what way is this a model of what is happening in the Earth?

Types of plate margins

Where convection brings hot rocks near to the surface, there is melting and magma forms. New volcanic rocks are added to the oceanic plate (site A, Figure 16.2). At site B, the oceanic plate sinks below the thicker continental plate, to become part of the mantle again. Lighter (less dense) layers of sediment on top of the oceanic plate buckle and fold upwards, and are added to the continental landmass nearby. There are three main kinds of plate margin (Figure 16.3).

Constructive margins
Here plates are moving apart as magma wells up from the mantle to form new oceanic crust. The Earth's surface area is increased.

Destructive margins
Plates are moving towards each other. As they collide the weaker plate sinks beneath the other. Surface area is lost.

Conservative margins
Two plates slip sideways along huge deep cracks called **transform** faults. Surface area is neither lost nor gained from either plate. The San Andreas fault that runs through San Francisco, USA, is one example of such a fault. Also see Figure 16.8.
- Find out the names of the two plates on either side of the San Andreas fault.

Sea-floor spreading

The world's ocean ridges are found at all constructive plate margins, wherever two plates are moving away from each other. They mark the sites where new plate material is being formed and added to existing plates. The movement of the plates away from the ocean ridges and the creation of new ocean floor is called **sea-floor spreading**. Volcanic activity is the main process. Although there are also earthquakes, they are usually slight.

Case study: Iceland

Iceland is a volcanic island that lies on the mid-Atlantic ridge. The island is being pulled apart and is widening at the rate of 2 cm a year as more and more crustal rock is formed (Figure 16.4). The youngest rocks in Iceland are found along the central zone. They have all formed in the last 20 000 years. Away from the central zone, rocks are progressively older.

Activity 16.4

Pillow lavas in wax

Using a lighted candle, investigate how melted wax forms pillow structures as it flows down the side of a candle. Try varying the cooling conditions for the wax.
1. What shape are the globules of wax if they run down the candle and cool at room temperature?
2. What structures form in the wax if the candle is set in a dish of cold water so that the wax flows into the water?
3. What happens if the wax flows into a dish of hot water?
4. In each case, explain fully why the globules of wax are the shape that they are. How do your results relate to true pillow lavas? **WP**

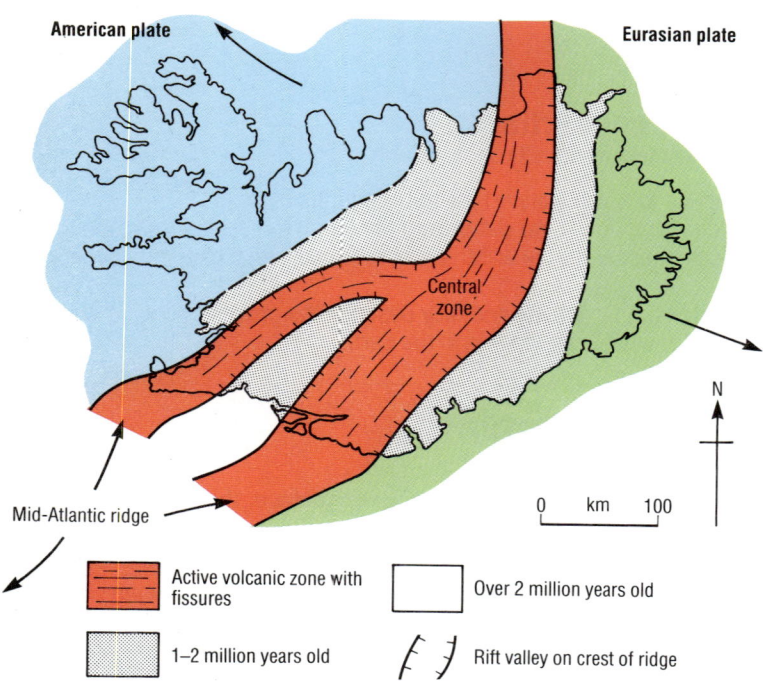

Figure 16.4 Map of Iceland

Figure 16.5 Pillow lavas

The ocean floor

Most of the volcanic activity happens on the sea-floor. There are many long **fissures** (cracks) erupting huge amounts of lava. The lava almost instantly hardens on contact with cold seawater to form layer after layer of structures called **pillows** (Figure 16.5). Each 'bubble' of lava forms a hard outer crust but the pressure of hot lava breaks through the 'bubble' to form a new structure which again instantly hardens.

A study of the ocean floor on either side of all ocean ridges shows a symmetrical pattern of magnetic stripes. As magma hardens to become an igneous rock, small iron crystals in the magma line up in the direction of the North magnetic pole. At intervals during the Earth's history, the North and South magnetic poles have suddenly changed round. These reversals are recorded as symmetrical stripes either side of the ridge (Figure 16.6).

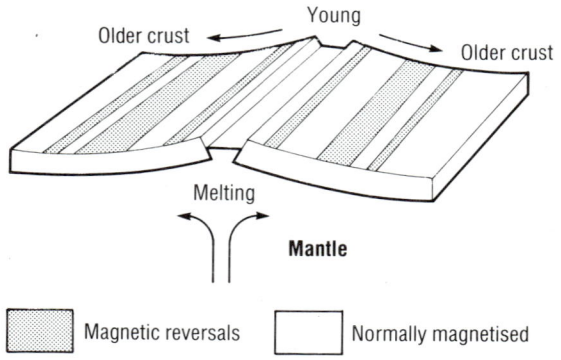

Figure 16.6 Symmetrical stripes on an ocean ridge

Summary

What are plates and how do they move and change shape? The theory of plate tectonics helps to explain why continents move, why there are earthquakes and volcanoes, and the formation of fold and block mountains.

What happens when plates collide?

These are the destructive plate margins where the weaker plate sinks beneath the other in a process called **subduction**. This happens at the ocean trenches – the deepest parts of the ocean floor. The Marianas trench in the Pacific Ocean is over 11 km deep (Figure 16.7). In this case, a thin oceanic plate sinks beneath another oceanic plate. As it does so there are earthquakes, and melting of rocks because of friction. The magma produces chains of volcanic islands known as **island arcs** (eg Japan).

Sometimes a thin oceanic plate sinks under a continental plate. Where this happens there will still be earthquakes and volcanoes. Sediments will also be scraped off and folded to form mountain ranges. The Nazca plate has slipped below South America to form the Andes mountains.

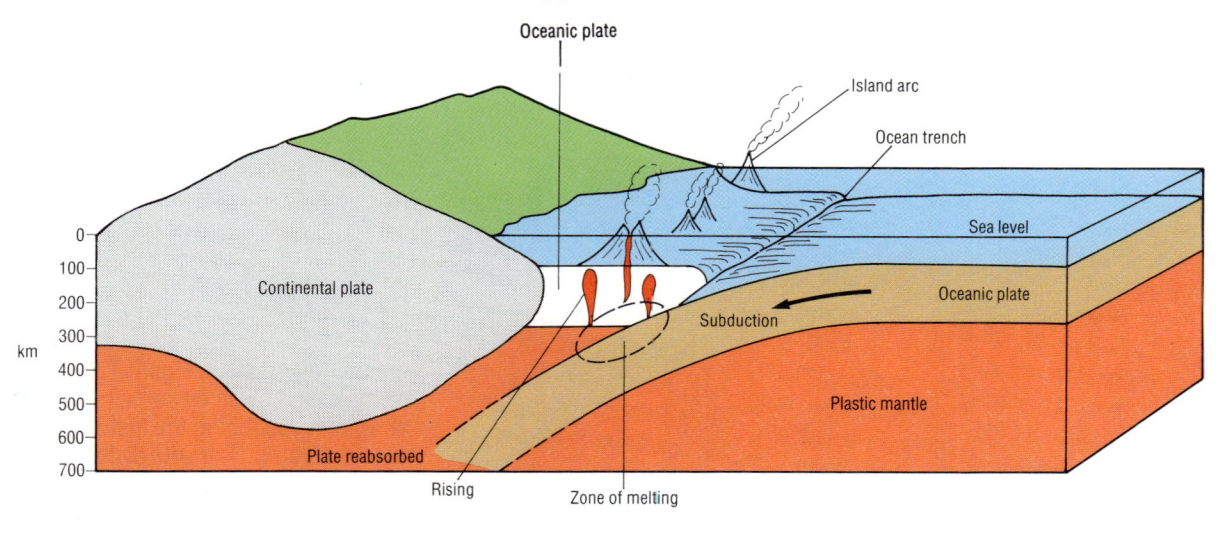

Figure 16.7 Oceanic plate returns to the mantle. Rising magma produces volcanic islands

When plates slide past each other

There are many places where plates are sliding past each other along **transform** faults like the San Andreas. Most transform faults cut across the ocean floor. Movement along such faults is often sudden and jerky, and large earthquakes are a constant threat.

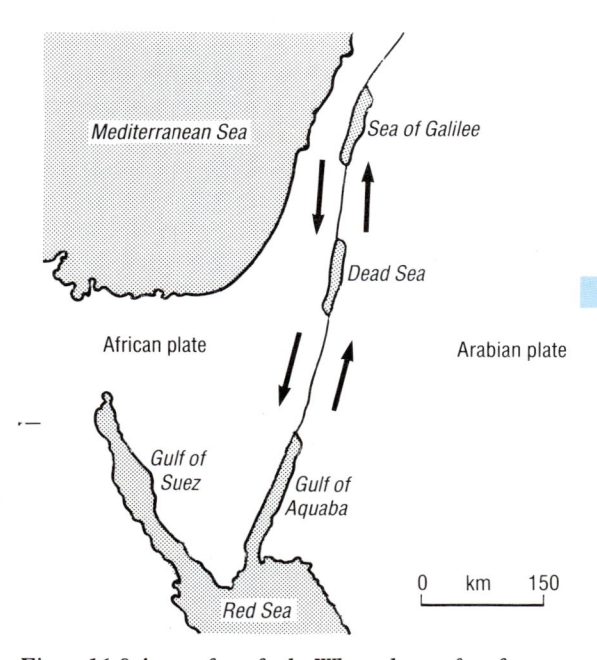

Figure 16.8 A transform fault. What other surface features have formed because of the fault movement?

Questions

1. Write out and complete the following statements using the words in brackets below.
   a Plate tectonics is the theory that there are a number of rigid .... called plates.
   b The plates move in response to ...... in the plastic mantle below.
   c There are few earthquakes or volcanoes in the ...... of plates. Most tectonic activity takes place at plate ....
   d A crack along which rocks move is called a ....
   e Folding, faulting and earthquakes are all the result of ...... processes.
   f Plates are moving about .... on average.
   (edges, segments, 6 cm/year, convection, centres, fault, tectonic)
2. Name two plates which do not have any continental crust.
3. Where are earthquakes more severe – along ocean trenches or ridges?
4. What fault type is produced by two plates sliding past each other?

Unit 17
Reading the rocks

How do we know that it has taken millions of years for rocks to form on the Earth? What were the early ideas about the Earth? How can fossils be used to date rock layers?

Early ideas

The scholars of ancient Greece knew that fossils were records of early life. By medieval times in Europe much of this early knowledge was forgotten. There were many legends to explain the existence of fossils.

Archbishop James Ussher (1581 – 1656). By the seventeenth century most people accepted Ussher's interpretation of the Old Testament and worked out that the Earth began in 4004 BC. Fossilised sea-shells found in rocks at the summits of mountains were explained away as having got there during Noah's flood, dated at 2348 BC.

James Hutton (1726 – 97), a Scottish farmer, realised that landscapes were eroded to form new sediments. He studied great thicknesses of sedimentary rocks and realised that their formation must have taken a very long time. He could see how slow erosive processes were. He thought they must have happened in the past at the same rate. He believed that 'the present was the key to the past', and was the first person to describe the **rock cycle** (see Unit 10).

Figure 17.1 Layers of sandstone and shale

Activity 17.1

The four diagrams in Figure 17.2 show the main events experienced by some rock layers. Write a paragraph describing the history recorded by these diagrams. The **unconformity** shown in (d) is an old erosion surface. This later became the sea-floor, before finally being uplifted. This unconformity line alone is likely to represent millions of years of Earth history. **WP**

Figure 17.2 History in the rocks

The time factor

Look at the layers in Figure 17.1. These layers were formed on the sea-floor. Not only must time be allowed for the layers to collect on the seabed, but they have to harden, and be uplifted and steeply tilted before erosion.

- From what you know of erosion, try to explain the jagged skyline.

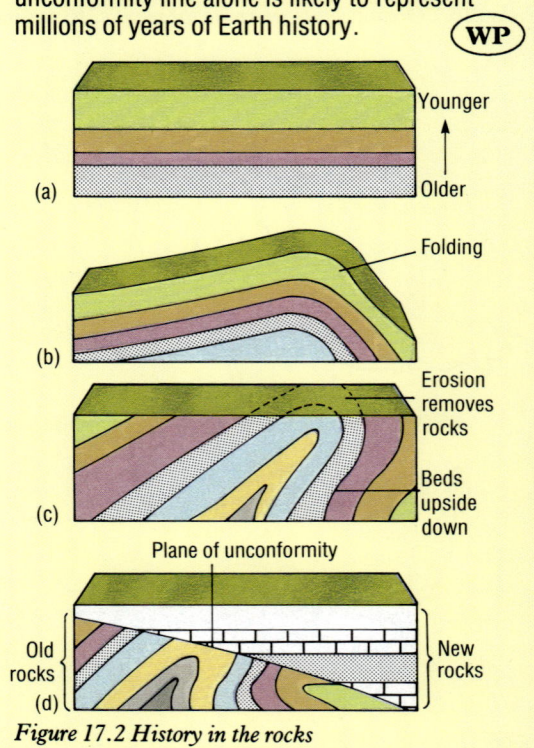

Matching up rocks with fossils

Sedimentary rocks are usually deposited as level layers in time order, so that older beds are at the bottom of the sequence. William Smith (1769 – 1839), a canal engineer, was one of the first people to realise how useful fossils could be in helping to sort out the time order of rock layers. Smith studied rocks alongside the new canals and collected the fossils he found in them. He noticed that each layer had its own particular fossils, some of which were only found in that layer and no other. These **index** fossils were evidence of organisms that had lived a short time before becoming extinct. He used them as age markers.

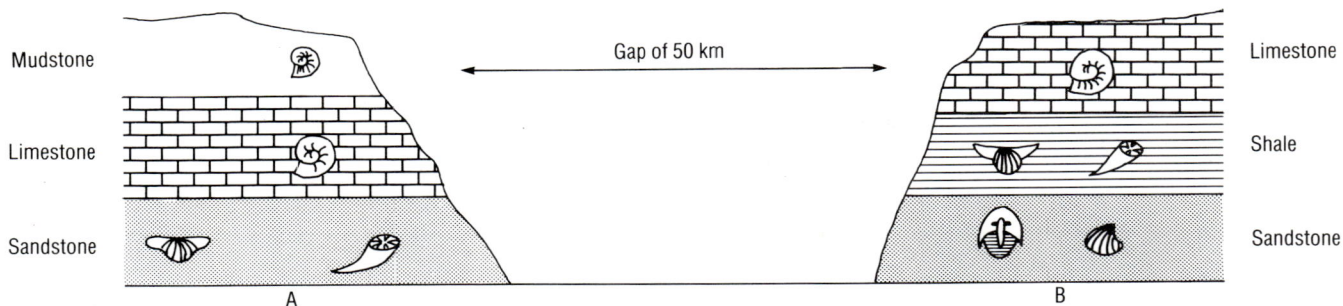

Figure 17.3 Matching up rocks

Activity 17.2

Look at Figure 17.4 and try to match up the rock layers using fossils.
1 Copy Figure 17.4 labelling the oldest rock 'a', the next oldest 'b', and so on.
2 Draw lines to connect rocks of the same age.

Smith found that it was easy to match up rocks of the same age found in different places using index fossils. For example, he noticed that a rock layer of the same age might be limestone in one place and sandstone in another. Look at Figure 17.3. The two sandstones at A and B seem to match up but the index fossils in each layer are different.

- If you follow the fossils, what is the correct way to match them?
- Make your own sketch of Figure 17.3 and use lines to join up layers of the same age.

Using this technique, Smith was able to work out the relative age of one layer compared to another and he classified all the rocks in Southern England. Activity 17.2 will show you how to do this.

Figure 17.4 Exercise to match up rocks

The matching of rocks by the use of index fossils is used today in the search for new deposits of coal and oil. Oil is often trapped by impermeable layers above anticlines, so it is important to know the structure (see Figure 17.5).

Activity 17.3

Look at Figure 17.5. At borehole A, two index fossil layers (X and Y) were found. Sandstone was struck at a depth of 300 m. It contained traces of oil. Index fossil X was also found at the surface. Index fossil bands were also found in borehole B.
1 Copy Figure 17.5 and mark in the shape of the sandstone structure.
2 Mark in a third drilling well where the sandstone is nearest to the surface.
3 What is the depth in metres to the top of the oil deposit?

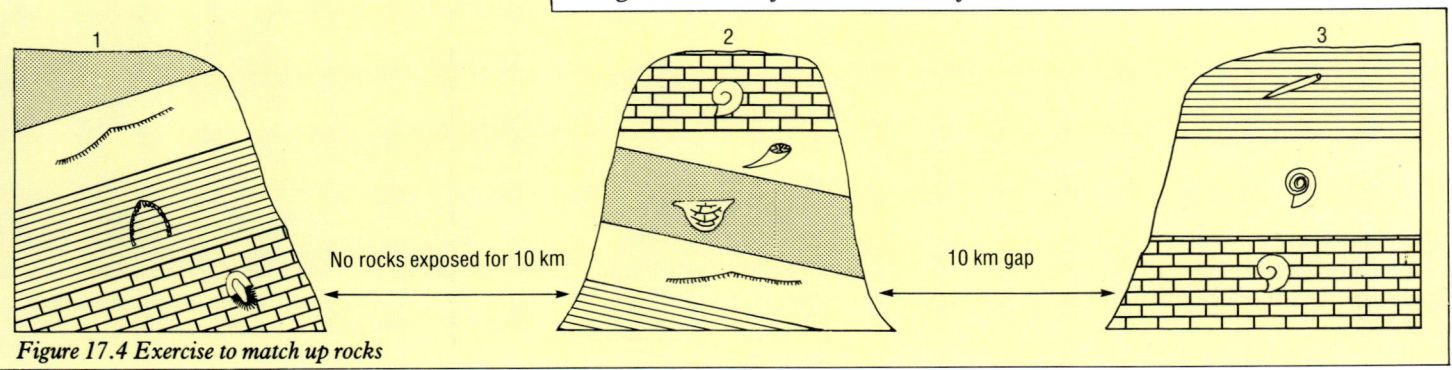

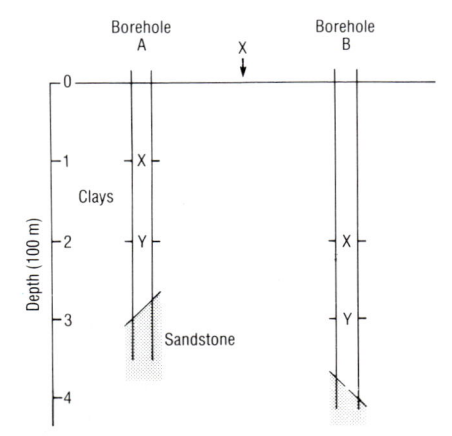

Figure 17.5 Finding the structure of the rock

Questions

1 What did Hutton mean by 'the present is the key to the past'?
2 What is an unconformity?
3 What is an index fossil?
4 Fully explain the uses of fossils.

Summary

Ideas about the age of the Earth have changed as more evidence has been found. We now know that rocks are millions of years old. Fossils give important clues to the age of rock layers.

Unit 18
The salty sea

Why is the sea so salty? What are the salts in seawater? The oceans cover 71% of the Earth's surface. They contain an estimated 1286 million cubic kilometres of water.

The salty sea

Seawater is salty because many dissolved minerals are added to seawater by rivers. 73% of the elements that occur naturally in the Earth's crust are found in seawater, but most are in tiny concentrations. For example, there is one hundred times more gold in seawater than on land but it is very diluted – 0.000004 parts per million. This makes it too expensive to extract.

Where do salts come from?

Salts come from the break-down of rocks on the land and from volcanoes. On average, every 1 kg of seawater contains about 35 g of dissolved minerals, of which 30 g is sodium chloride (common salt) (Figure 18.1).

Strangely, the oceans are not getting any saltier. This is because minerals settle out as layers on the seabed. Substances like calcium bicarbonate are extracted from seawater and used by living organisms to make shells, coral stems and other hard skeletal parts. Sodium chloride is not used by sea-living organisms. It therefore forms the main substance in seawater.

Figure 18.1 Collecting dried sea salt. Why is this activity only seen in countries with a hot, dry climate?

Activity 18.1 Dissolved substances in seawater   CP

In 35 g of dissolved salts, 4.5 g are sulphates of magnesium, potassium and calcium. Expressed as a percentage, this is 13% ((4.5/35) × 100%).
1 Given that in 35 g of salts, 30 g are sodium chloride, calculate its percentage in the same way.
2 Construct a pie-chart to show these figures and label it. There is also a small percentage of trace elements in seawater which you can label on your graph.

Have salts ever been deposited in Britain?

In hot, dry climates, so much water can evaporate from shallow seas that evaporite rocks are deposited. Saline rocks are forming today near the Red Sea and the Dead Sea in Israel. This could never happen in our climate, yet thick deposits of salt and rocks with desert sandstones are found in much of Britain (Figure 18.2).

Figure 18.2 shows the British area 250 million years ago. There was a shallow inlet from the Permian Sea from which water evaporated. 250 million years ago, Britain was much farther south than it is today. It had a hot, dry climate. Up to 25 m of salts were deposited at that time. They are now being mined in Cheshire.

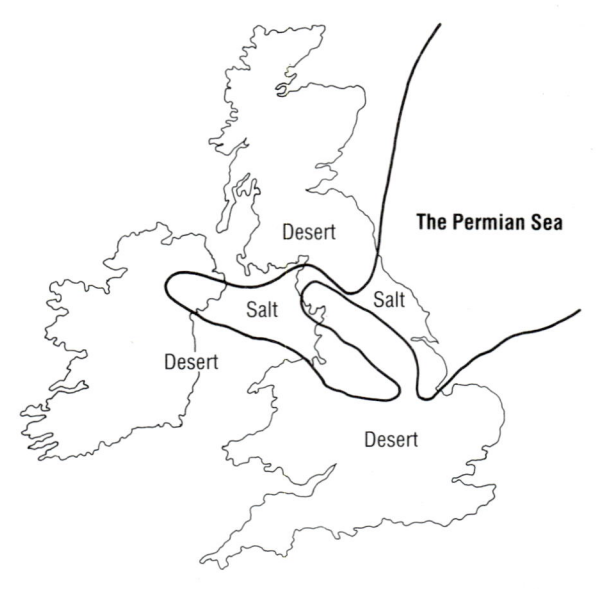

Figure 18.2 The British area 250 million years ago. There was a shallow inlet from the Permian Sea from which water evaporated

Activity 18.3

Is the seawater deposit mainly sodium chloride?

Test the deposit you got from the seawater in a flame, using a flame wire (see Figure 18.4). If the flame turns yellow, it means that sodium is present.

1. Dip the test wire into hydrochloric acid to clean it and heat in a strong Bunsen flame.
2. Dip the wire in the deposit.
3. Hold the test wire in the flame of the Bunsen burner. What colour does the flame turn?
4. Try this test again, this time using a known solution of sodium chloride. Is the flame the same colour this time?
5. Now dissolve the remainder of the deposit in distilled water and add a drop of silver nitrate solution. If a chloride is present a white solid will settle out from the solution. Is this what happens?
6. Repeat 5 using the sodium chloride solution. Do you get the same result?
7. Write down and fully explain all your results.

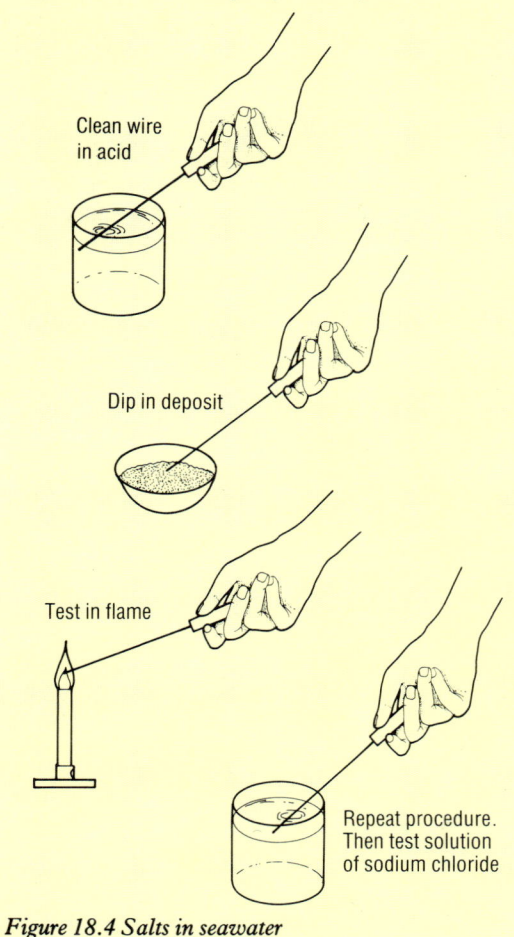

Figure 18.4 Salts in seawater

Activity 18.2

Salts in seawater

Fill an evaporating dish with seawater and record its weight. Then heat it until the water boils away. Reweigh the dish.

Calculate the amount of salt that was in your seawater sample – is this figure the same as the percentage you worked out in Activity 18.1? Try this with river water for comparison. Do you get the same results? Explain why.

Salinity and density

Salinity is the degree of saltiness of the water. The average volume of dissolved substances in seawater is between 33 and 37 parts per 1000. This means that seawater has a salinity of 3.3 – 3.7%. Salinity varies from place to place – some seas are much saltier than others. The Baltic Sea is in an area with high rainfall and receives fresh water from the rivers, so its salinity is 0.72%. In contrast, the Dead Sea is in a hot desert climate and has a high salinity. Highly saline water is much denser than water with a low salinity. Would it be easier to float in the Baltic Sea or the Dead Sea? Differences in the density of seawater affect the circulation and movement of the ocean currents.

Figure 18.3 Why is it so easy to float in the Dead Sea?

Summary

The seas and oceans contain many dissolved substances, deposited by rivers. How do these salts eventually get deposited? Landlocked tropical seas are saltier because evaporation is greater than the supply of fresh water.

Questions

1. Give two reasons why seawater is salty.
2. Explain why the oceans are not getting any saltier.
3. What is the main salt found in seawater?
4. Why isn't gold extracted from seawater in the same way as sodium chloride?
5. What is meant by salinity? Why does salinity vary from place to place?
6. Why is the Dead Sea far more salty than average seawater?

Unit 19
The moving sea

Did you know that all the water in the oceans is constantly moving? If this movement did not happen, then there would not be enough dissolved oxygen in the water for all the fish and other forms of life. Did you know that ocean currents control the world's climates?

Water moves in three main ways: waves, tides and ocean currents.

Waves

Most waves are caused by winds blowing across open sea. The height of a wave is the distance between its trough and crest. The height increases as winds get stronger. In a storm, waves may reach heights of 12 m or more.

How waves move

In the open sea, waves move water particles in a rotating circular motion. This gets less with depth, so waves are only movements of water quite close to the surface (Figure 19.2). The circular motion means that a floating object like a small boat will bob up and down, rather than sideways. As a wave comes into shallower water near the beach, the lower part drags against the seabed. This flattens the circular motion and finally the top of the wave falls over. The wave then becomes a **breaker** as the water surges forward up the shore – much to the joy of surfers!

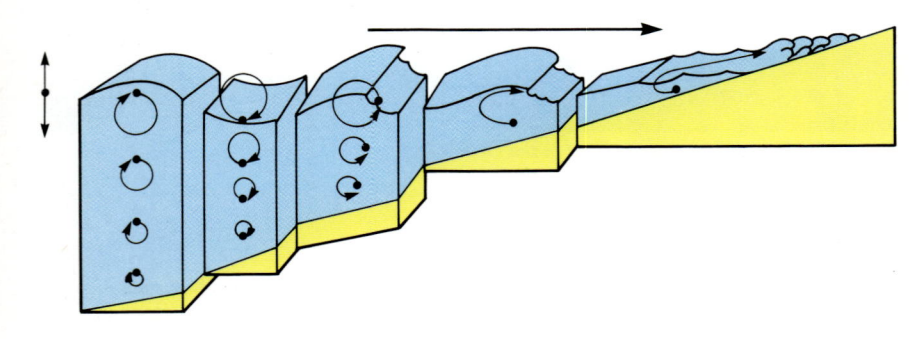

Figure 19.2 Orbital motion of water particles in waves

Tides

Tides are rises and falls in the level of the oceans. Tidal currents can be very strong, especially in narrowing estuaries, where the difference between low and high tide is about 12 m. In enclosed seas, like the Mediterranean, there is hardly any tidal movement. The causes of tides are explained more fully in Unit 29.

Figure 19.1 Surfers love breakers

Activity 19.1

Water movements
Set up a shallow tray as a ripple tank (Figure 19.3). Place a weighted wedge of wood in the tank to act as a model shoreline. Then make waves by moving another piece of wood backwards and forwards. Sprinkle chalk dust on the water to see how surface currents move.
1 Make a sketch map to record the movements. Study bottom currents by placing a few crystals of potassium permanganate in the tank. As the water moves, watch the patterns made by the purple dye.
2 Make a sketch map of the movement.
3 Compare the two sketches you have made – is there any difference in the way surface and bottom currents move?

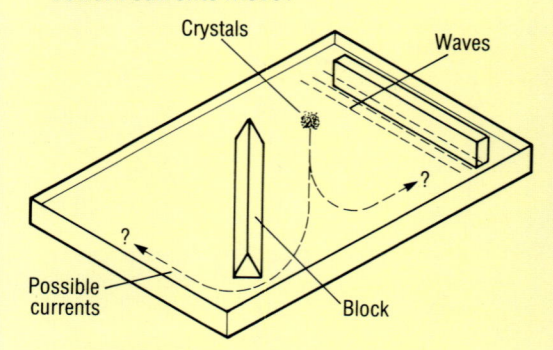

Figure 19.3 Studying water movement

Tsunamis

The fastest and most destructive sea waves of all are **tsunamis** which are caused by earthquakes or explosive volcanic eruptions on the seabed.

Figure 19.4 shows the time it took (in hours) for a tsunami from Alaska to cross the Pacific Ocean in 1964. Giant waves over 10 m high hit the coast near Alaska, carrying boats several kilometres inland. The waves were still 7 m high as they moved south down the coast of California. Hawaii recorded waves 2 m high. The danger from tsunamis in the Pacific is so great that a station based in Hawaii relays warnings of approaching waves to countries likely to be affected. Tsunamis have a wavelength (the distance between two crests) of hundreds of kilometres, but their height in the open ocean is no more than 1 m. Ships are often unaware of them. The whole depth of ocean is involved in the wave motion of a tsunami. As the wave reaches a shallowing shoreline, its height increases up to 20 – 30 m (Figure 19.5).

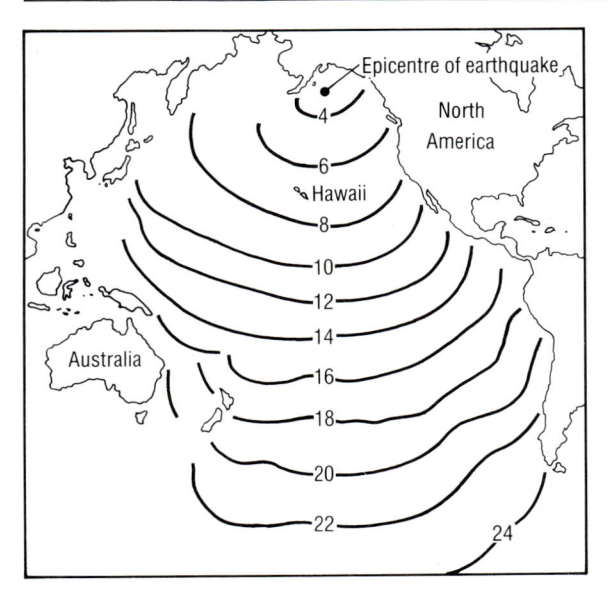

Figure 19.4 The time taken in hours for the Alaskan tsunami wave to cross the Pacific Ocean, a distance of 15 000 km

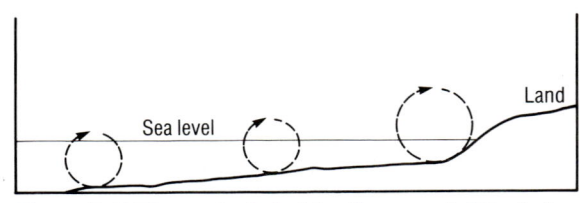

Figure 19.5 Changes in the height of a tsunami. Why is the wave height greater at the shore?

Activity 19.2 Tsunamis

Look at Figure 19.4.
1. How long did it take for the tsunami to reach the coast of Australia?
2. What part of Australia do you think had the highest waves – west, north, north-east or south? Give reasons for your answer.
3. Why were the waves so high near Alaska?
4. How long did it take for the wavefronts to cross the Pacific Ocean, from north to south?
5. Work out the wave velocity in kilometres per hour.

Ocean currents

No part of the oceans are completely still. Even at great depths there is a slow movement of water. The surface waters of the oceans are moved by winds. (You can refer to a good atlas to see the pattern of ocean currents.) The warmest water is near the equator where the oceans receive most of the Sun's heat. Water flows from the tropics towards the poles. Water from the poles is heavier because it is colder. It sinks under the warm water and flows towards the equator. The circulation pattern is affected by the shapes of the land masses, just as it was in the ripple-tank activity.

Ocean currents and climate

The warm current in the North Atlantic is called the **Gulf Stream** or **North Atlantic Drift**. The presence of this current means that winds blowing over the North Atlantic often give Britain and Northern Europe mild winters and cool summers. Places at the same distance from the North Pole as Britain in North America are snow-bound for several months. Ocean currents therefore have an important effect on weather and climate.

Questions

1. A friend tells you he has decided to go surfing in the middle of the ocean. He argues that the waves are bound to be better farther out. Do you agree with him? Write a letter to him explaining why he might be wrong. **WP**
2. Draw a scaled sketch to show the relative heights of tsunamis compared to ordinary waves.
3. Why are tsunamis so dangerous?
4. Fully describe the motion of ocean waves.
5. How does the North Atlantic Drift affect our weather?
6. What would happen to our climate if the North Atlantic Drift suddenly became a cold current?

Summary

The seas and oceans of the world are in constant motion. Waves, tides and ocean currents cause these movements, which can have some far-reaching effects on people and on the climate.

Unit 20
Ocean floor deposits

The oceans form a vast area of our planet. It is only recently that they have been studied in any detail. The oceans have great future economic importance. As mineral ores on land run out, it will be necessary to look for them in the sea.

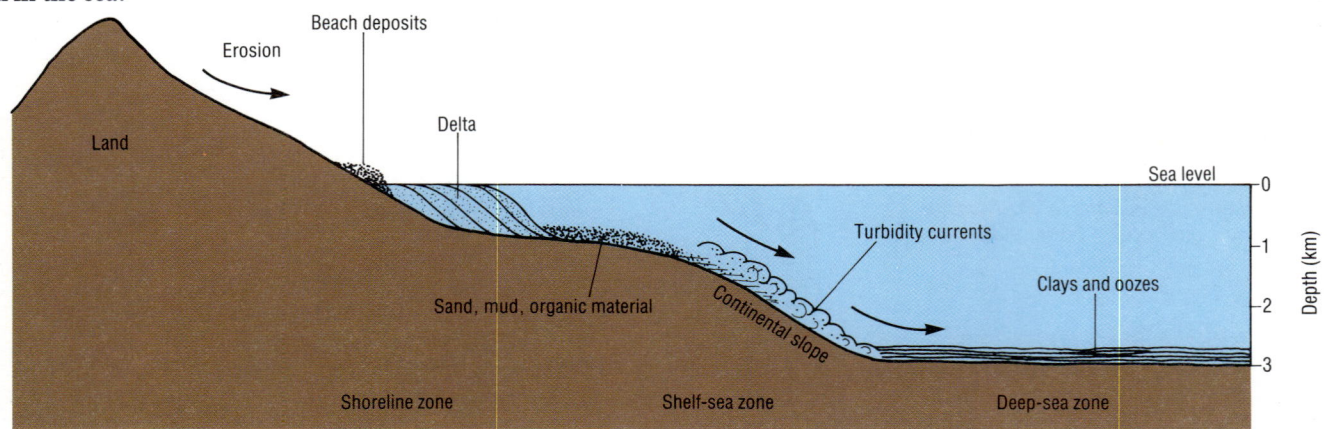

Figure 20.1 Sediments on the ocean floor

Deposits

Much of the eroded material from the land is deposited on the sea-floor and forms new sedimentary rocks. Usually the coarser material is dropped near to the shore. Some of the environments of deposition are shown in Figure 20.1. In the shoreline zone, deposits of pebbles and sand are common. They form beaches and deltas. Waves and tidal movements tend to sort and distribute this material. A typical sorted deposit is a coarse pebbly beach, grading to finer sand and mud.

Turbidity currents

Much of the loose material on the continental shelf will be dislodged by earthquakes and roll down the slope in a dense cloud. These huge underwater avalanches are known as **turbidity currents**. The clay and sand from them settles out on the deep sea-floor to form an unsorted mixture called **greywacke**.

Coral reefs

In many clear shallow tropical seas there are coral reefs. A coral is a small animal which often lives in large colonies, where it builds up a reef structure. Corals remove calcium bicarbonate from the seawater and use it to make the reef structure on which they live. Coral reefs grow best in shallow water, but can be found down to a depth of about 60 m. Many islands and coastlines are fringed by coral. The Great Barrier Reef off the East coast of Australia stretches for thousands of kilometres along the shoreline and is so large that it is visible from outer space. Fossil reefs are found in many rock sequences and are important as rock builders.
- What kind of rock will a coral reef form?

Activity 20.1
Looking at rocks

1. Use a hand lens to examine a sample of greywacke and compare it to a quartz sandstone. You should be able to see that the grains of sand are set in a fine clay cement. How does it compare with the quartz sandstone (Figure 20.2)?
2. Compare a piece of reef coral with a sample of reef limestone containing corals. Test both samples with dilute hydrochloric acid to find out if they both are calcium carbonate. What is the reaction?

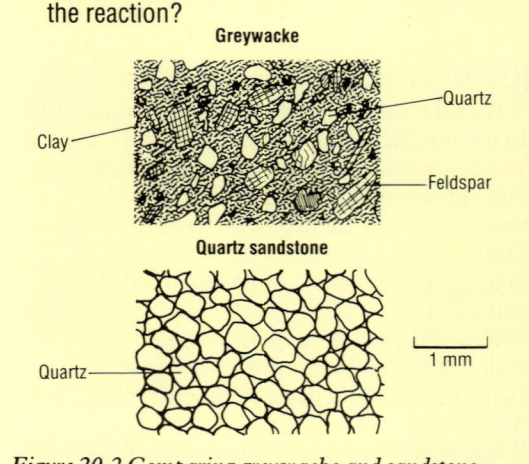

Figure 20.2 Comparing greywacke and sandstone

Clays and oozes

Few animals can live at a depth of 4000 m on the deep ocean floor. Not only is the water very cold but it is also completely dark. The remains of tiny floating animals and plants settle to form the fine muds known as **oozes**. **Red clay** is another deep-sea deposit. It is formed from volcanic ash, dust from outer space and material brought by icebergs.

Metallic nodules and smoker vents

Lumps of iron, manganese and nickel are also found everywhere on the deep ocean floor. They are known as **nodules** (Figure 20.3). Each nodule is about the size and shape of a potato. They also contain copper and cobalt. It is estimated that tens of millions of square kilometres are covered with nodules. These have great future potential as a source of metal ores.

Recently mineral deposits have been discovered around cracks in the rocks of the ocean floor. These 'smoker' vents (Figure 20.4) produce a mixture of volcanic gases and hot black sulphurous water containing many dissolved minerals. The sulphur from these vents reacts with seawater. Bacteria can feed on the sulphides that are produced and giant clams and tube worms live on the bacteria in complete darkness.

Figure 20.3 Metallic nodules

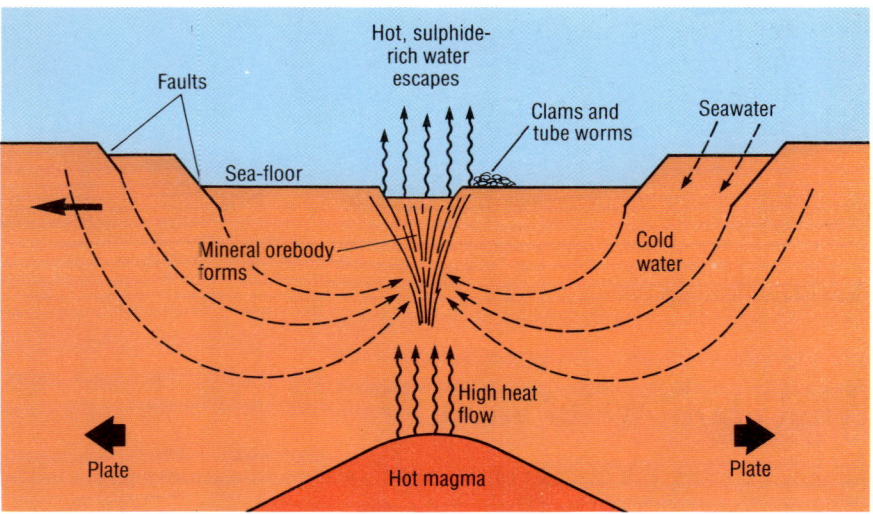

Figure 20.4 A 'smoker' vent

How do smoker vents form?

The vents are produced above bodies of hot magma, at places where the crust is being pulled apart by plate movements (Figure 20.4). This is very like the process which formed mineral veins of tin and other metals above the hot granite intrusion in Cornwall discussed in Unit 2.

Heat from the magma sets up a convective circulation of water. Cold water is drawn in through the surrounding rocks. It is then heated and passes out through the smoker vents. Large amounts of dissolved minerals then crystallize on the sides of the crack or mineral vein. This process explains how elements like gold, which are present in such tiny amounts in seawater, can become concentrated in vein deposits. Copper, zinc, silver, cadmium and cobalt have all been found at vent sites.

Summary

The ocean floor is a busy place – not only is it affected by deposits of new sediments but by other processes such as hot sulphide springs and the formation of metallic nodules.

Questions

1. What are the various processes of sediment formation on the sea-floor?
2. You are working for an exploration company looking for new minerals using a mini-submarine. Write a report about your new mineral finds. **WP**
3. Explain how volcanic activity and plate movements can lead to the formation of orebodies on the sea-floor.
4. 'All life depends on the Sun as its energy source.' What does this statement mean? Why is it no longer absolutely true?

Unit 21
Water on the land

Did you know that the total amount of water on Earth is an amazing 1360 million cubic kilometres and nearly all of this is in the oceans? Did you know that the **hydrological** (water) cycle is kept going by the Sun's heat?

The Sun's heat causes **evaporation** of moisture from the oceans. Only a tiny fraction of water is evaporated, yet it is enough to provide cloud and rain over much of the world (Figure 21.1).

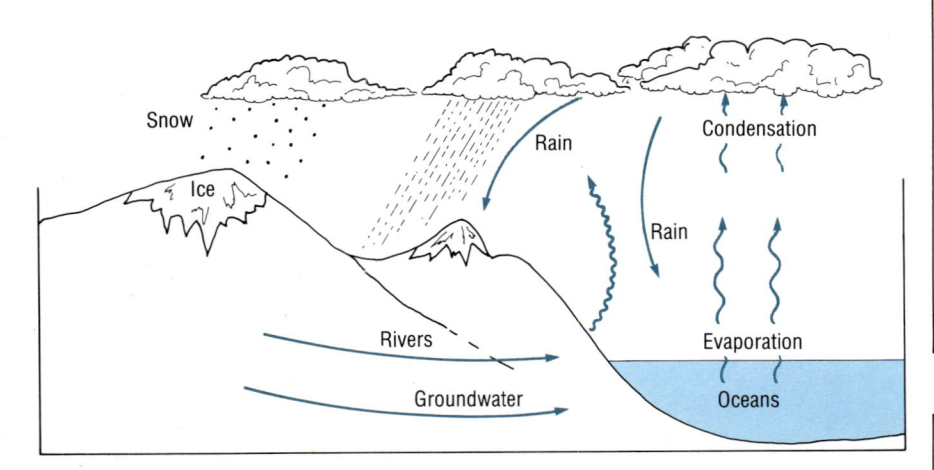

Figure 21.1 The water cycle

What about water vapour?

The environment with the least of the world's water is the atmosphere. Only about one hundredth of 1% of the world's water exists as a gas. This is the water vapour in the air. Although this sounds a tiny amount, the evaporation is taking place from the whole of the Earth's surface. Every year, 500 000 cubic kilometres of water evaporates to become water vapour. This gas rises and then **condenses** (liquifies) as it cools, to form tiny water droplets in the clouds. When it rains or snows, most of the moisture returns directly into the sea. Air movements carry some of it over the land.

Are we getting enough?

Compared to the amount of rainfall received by the oceans, it might not seem as if the land gets all that much. In fact the continents receive around 40 000 cubic kilometres of rain every year. Unfortunately the rain does not fall equally over the whole land area. 32% of the land surface is desert and therefore too dry for many forms of life. Also 17% is either frozen or under ice.

Activity 21.1

Where is the world's water?
The table below shows where the world's water can be found.

Location	Percentage
Oceans	97.0
Ice-sheets	2.0
Groundwater	0.5
Lakes and rivers	0.5

1 Display these figures in a divided bar graph.
2 Where is most of the world's water?

CP

Activity 21.2

Study Figure 21.2. Make a list of all the different parts of the water cycle that you can see.

Figure 21.2 How many parts of the water cycle can you see?

Activity 21.3

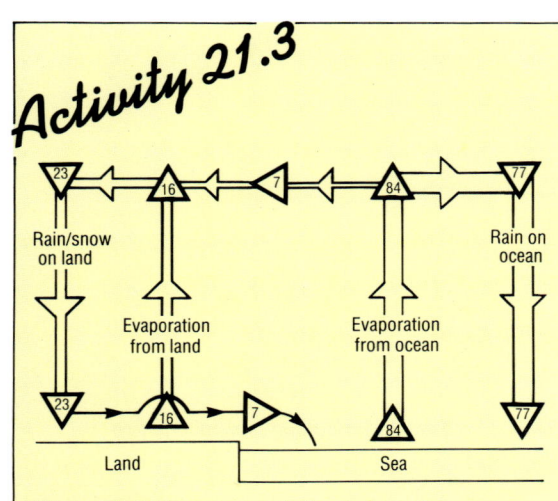

Figure 21.3 The water cycle is a balanced system. (The figures are given as percentages)

How does the water cycle work? CP
Look carefully at Figure 21.3. It shows how water moves through the cycle. Answer the following questions.
1. Where is the most evaporation – from the land or the sea? Draw a pie-chart to show this difference.
2. What percentage of water vapour is carried sideways over the land? Notice how this figure is balanced by the loss of water from the land caused by river flow.
3. Where does most rain fall – over the land or the sea? Draw a pie-chart to show this. CP

What happens to moisture that falls on land?

Of all the water that falls as rain or snow on the land, 75% is stored in glaciers and polar icecaps. The rocks and the soil hold 24.5% as **groundwater** and the final 0.5% is fresh water held in lakes and rivers.

- Draw another pie-chart to display these figures. CP

How does rain become groundwater?

Some rainwater soaks through the soil into the rocks, where it becomes groundwater. Soil is composed of grains of broken-down rock mixed with humus – the decayed remains of plants. Between the grains there are air spaces and water soaks into these spaces. The rate at which it does this depends on:

(a) the size of the spaces,
(b) how moist the soil is initially.

Soil or rocks which allow water to pass through them easily are **permeable**. Fine-grained rocks and soil have fewer air spaces and are therefore **impermeable**. It is possible to measure the permeability of soil – that is, the rate at which water soaks into it.

- Which of the two soils in Figure 21.4 will allow water to pass through it the quickest? In other words, which is the most permeable? Explain your answer. You could test this by carrying out Activity 21.4.

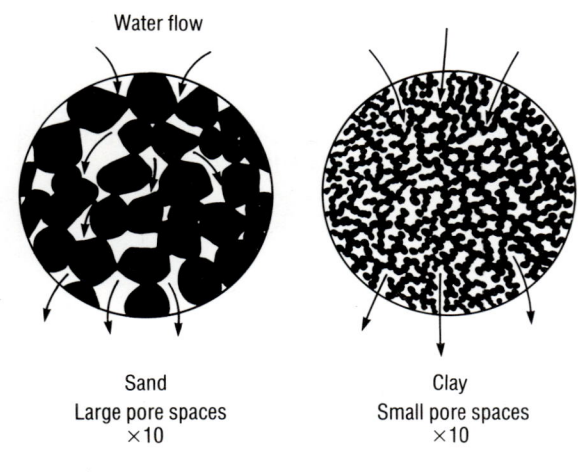

Figure 21.4 How water soaks into the soil. Which soil will allow the quickest seepage?

Activity 21.4

How fast does water soak into different soils?
Think of a way to compare the permeability rates of different soils by testing samples of sand, clay and loam. Loam is a more evenly textured soil with coarse and fine grains.
1. Allow a known amount of water to filter through each sample.
2. Record the time it takes for water to pass through each sample.
3. Make bar charts of your results to compare them and describe what you have found out. CP

Water in the rocks

Not all of the water passes through soil into the rocks below. Some is absorbed by plants and some evaporates directly.

Some rocks are more permeable than others. Sandstone is an example of a **porous** rock. It has a mass of tiny pores or air spaces through which water can pass. Other rocks such as limestone and granite do not have pores, but they are still permeable because water can flow through joints and cracks instead. Rocks such as shale, clay or mudstone are impermeable – they do not allow water to flow through them.

Activity 21.5

Fieldwork on permeability of soils
Soil samples tested in the laboratory have been loosened and disturbed, so the only real way to know their natural permeability is to test them in the field.
1 Cut both ends off a large catering tin can, taking care to avoid sharp edges (your teacher will show you how to do this safely).
2 Use a block of wood across the top of the can to push the tin into the soil to a depth of at least 6 cm. Choose a suitable site above undisturbed soil.
3 Pour 1 litre of water into the can and use a stopwatch to measure how long it takes for the water to soak away. When this has happened, repeat the procedure. Does the second litre soak away faster or more slowly? You can refine this technique. For example, if you place a millimetre ruler vertically in the can, it becomes possible to measure the soak-in rate in millimetres per hour.
4 Draw line graphs of your results (Figure 21.5). **CP**

Further work
Work in groups. Use the technique described above to carry out fieldwork of your own. For example, you might investigate the following questions.
1 Which site on the school field has the most permeable soil?
2 Is it true that water takes longer to soak in if the weather has been wet, compared to the rate after a dry spell?
3 How do soak-in rates compare at the same sites from winter to summer?

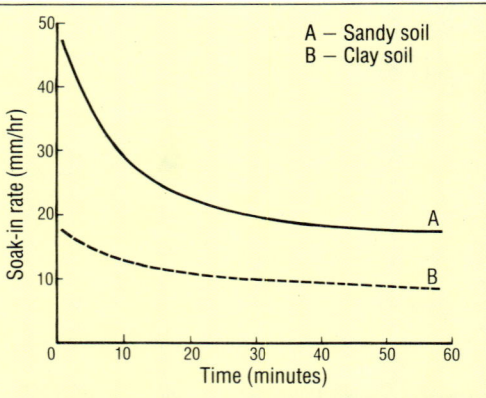

Figure 21.5 The rate of soaking compared in two different soils

Activity 21.6

Comparing graphs of soak-in rates
Look carefully at the graphs shown in Figure 21.5.
1 One line represents a clayey soil, the other line a sandy soil. Which is which? Give your reasons.
2 What is the highest rate shown for each soil?
3 Why does the soak-in rate drop after 10 minutes?

How is water stored?

Water-bearing layers of rock are called **aquifers**. When a permeable rock layer lies above an impermeable rock, groundwater cannot seep down any farther. Every available space is filled up and the rock becomes saturated. The top of the saturated zone is called the **water table**. In very wet weather the water table will be at a higher level than in dry weather. The water table normally follows the shape of the ground, curving upwards under hills and flattening out under plains (Figure 21.6).

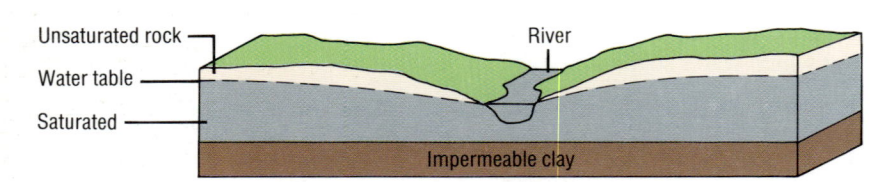

Figure 21.6 Water table and springs

How does water reach the surface again?

Wherever the water table reaches the surface, water flows out into springs, lakes or rivers.

If the aquifer is downfolded, the groundwater is often heated as water encounters warmer rocks at depth. The Romans made use of this when they discovered hot springs at Bath. The temperature of the spring water is 46.5 °C at the surface. This water fell on the Mendip Hills 15 km away. It takes 2000 years for the water to seep down through the limestone.

Activity 21.7

How much water do different rocks absorb?

Try this activity with samples of sandstone, shale, granite and limestone.

It is possible to find out how porous a rock is and therefore how much water it can hold, using the following formula:

$$\text{porosity (\%)} = \frac{\text{volume of water absorbed}}{\text{volume of rock}} \times 100\%$$

1. Fill a measuring cylinder with water up to the 50 ml mark and submerge the sample of rock.
2. Write down the total volume of water plus sample. Then subtract 50 from this figure to find the volume of the rock (Figure 21.7).
3. Leave the sample submerged for several hours to allow it to soak up water. If the rock is porous you will see air bubbles leaving the sample as they are displaced by the water.
4. Remove the sample from the water, without losing any water from the cylinder. Read off the water level in millilitres. If the rock is porous this reading will be lower because some of the water will have been absorbed.
5. Use this information to work out the percentage porosity of the sample.
6. Which of the rock samples soaks up the most water? Why do you think this is?
7. Write a short report describing what you have found out in this activity. **WP**

Figure 21.7 Apparatus for measuring the porosity of rocks

Activity 21.8

Look at Figure 21.8
1. What is the temperature of water as it soaks into the limestone on the Mendip Hills?
2. What is the highest temperature reached by the water?
3. Why does the water cool to 46.5 °C?
4. Why doesn't the water find other routes to the surface?

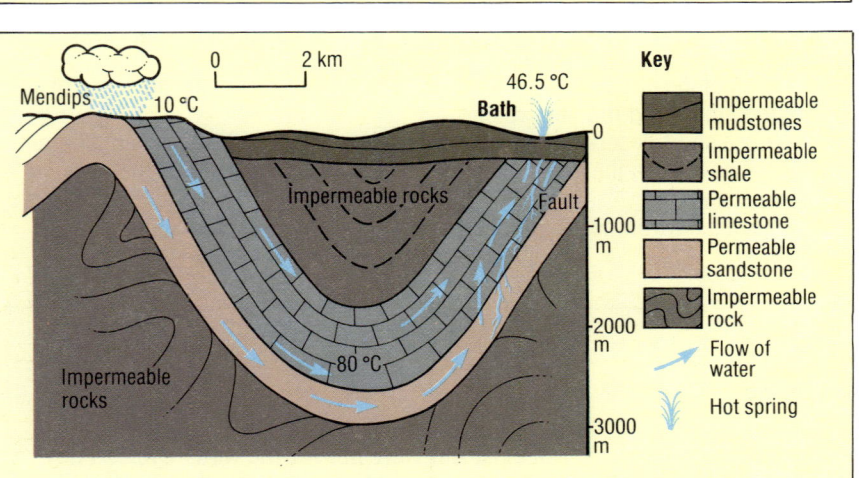

Figure 21.8 The hot springs at Bath. The permeable limestone and sandstone act like a huge pipe, and allow water to pass through them. They are sandwiched between impermeable rocks, above and below. Water is heated at depth. It then flows out along the fault line at Bath under pressure. The pressure is due to the greater height of the Mendips

Summary

How does the water cycle work? Much of the world's rainfall returns to the atmosphere by direct evaporation but some water soaks into the soil and the rocks, only to reach the surface again eventually as springs.

Questions

1. Explain how water circulates through the hydrological cycle (see Figures 21.1 and 21.2).
2. Show by means of a divided bar graph or pie-chart how much of the world's land area is suitable for most life, compared with the areas for deserts and ice.
3. Where is most of the moisture stored on land?
4. How does water penetrate soil and rocks?
5. What is groundwater and the water table?
6. Which of these soils is likely to be the most permeable:
   a a dry clay soil after a summer drought,
   b a sandy loam after a heavy rain.
   Give reasons for your answers.

Unit 22
The power of rivers

Running water has a big effect in shaping the Earth's landscapes. Deep river valleys are cut as water rushes downslope. This would not happen at all if it weren't for the continual movement of water through the water cycle – from ocean to atmosphere to land, and back to ocean again.

Activity 22.1

The Moon and the Earth

Compare photographs (a) and (b) in Figure 22.1. One photograph shows a landscape on the Moon's (lunar) surface, the other a landscape on Earth.

1. Which of the photographs shows a landscape formed in the presence of an atmosphere and running water?
2. Write a short description of each landscape. Why are they both so different?
3. What have been the main processes that have formed each of the landscapes?
4. In which environment might you find sedimentary rocks? Explain your answer.

Figure 22.1 (a) The surface of the Moon and (b) a landscape on Earth

Rivers

Streams and rivers would not exist if it were not for the water cycle. They carry water back to the sea from the land. The start of a river is called the **source**. For many rivers the source is a melting glacier or a spring where groundwater from rocks reaches the surface again.

The power of rivers

The downward flow of water under gravity gives rivers the power to cut steep-sided V-shaped valleys. Loose rocks and pebbles removed by erosion are picked up by the current. They collide with the bed and bank of the river to cause more downcutting and erosion.

Formation of potholes

Swirling river currents pick up pebbles and they are spun round in a corkscrew motion to form a circular hole in the solid rock of the river bed (Figure 22.3). Eventually the separate potholes widen and join together, and the whole stream bed is lowered.

Activity 22.2

Some facts about rivers

Here is a list of terms about rivers, and their meanings. Copy Figure 22.2 and label the boxes with the correct items:

Source – the point where a river begins.
Mouth – where a river flows into the sea.
Drainage basin – an area of land drained by a river system.
Watershed – the dividing line between one river basin and the next.
Delta – deposited material at the mouth of some rivers.
Estuary – a wide stretch of tidal river at the mouth.
Tributary – a small stream which joins a larger one.
Confluence – the point where two streams join.

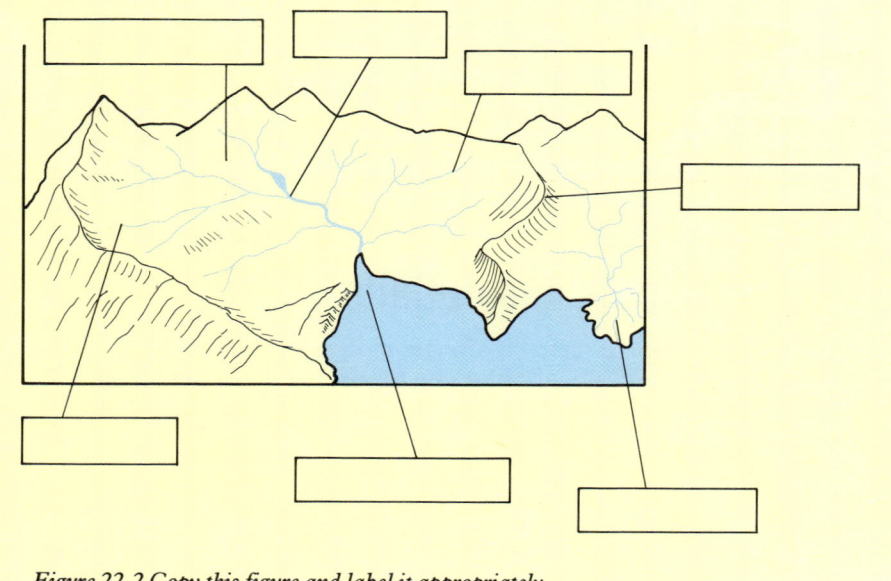

Figure 22.2 Copy this figure and label it appropriately

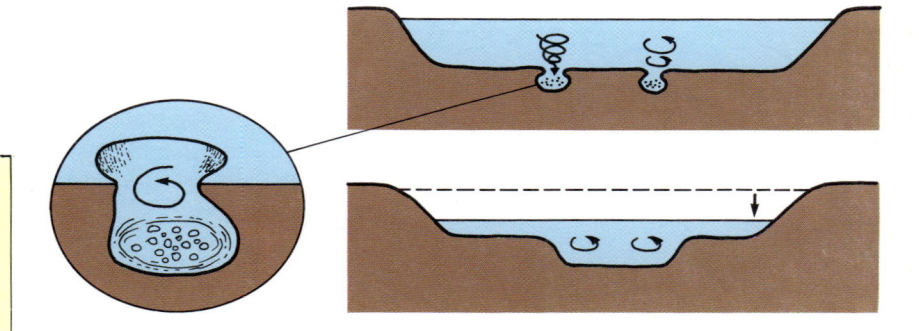

Figure 22.3 Pothole formation

Activity 22.3

The River Lune, Lancashire

Study Figure 22.4.
1 Was the photograph taken in summer or winter? Give your reasons.
2 What evidence is there that the river can flow faster and more deeply?
3 Make a labelled sketch of the photograph and label these features: pebble beach, inner bend, shallow bank, steep bank.
4 Explain what has happened for so much load to be deposited on the inner bend of the stream.

Figure 22.4 The River Lune, near Lancaster

Transport

The material carried by rivers is called its load. This consists of boulders, pebbles, sand and mud as well as dissolved material. Rivers transport their load in four main ways.

a In solution – dissolved chemicals are carried in the water.
b In suspension – silt, mud and fine sand are carried along without touching the river bed.
c In saltation – larger particles such as gravel bounce along the river bed in the current.
d In traction – larger pebbles and boulders roll and slide along.

Deposition

As a river nears its mouth, there is usually a shallower slope, so the current slows. The river begins to deposit its load. At the river mouth, the sediment may be carried away by ocean currents and tidal movements, or built out in layers to form a delta.

Inputs and outputs from a river system

It is possible to think of the whole of a drainage basin as a system where the *input* is the water received by rainfall and the *output* is the river water flowing from the basin to the sea. The whole drainage basin system with its many tributaries collects the rainfall and channels it towards the sea, where it is discharged. It follows from this that a small amount of rainfall could become concentrated as a large volume of water, once it flows into the river channels.

Measuring inputs and outputs

It is possible to calculate the amount of water received (the input) by collecting and measuring rainfall with a rain gauge. Just 1 mm of rain can produce a huge volume of water. Volume is measured in cubic metres (m^3). If each square kilometre (km^2) in a drainage basin receives 1 mm of rain, then the volume could be worked out as follows:

Volume of water (m^3) = area × rainfall
= 1 km^2 × 1 mm
= 1000 × 1000 × 0.001
= 1000 m^3

Activity 22.4

How does load settle?
River water is often cloudy when the stream is in flood.
1. Collect a sample of cloudy river water from your local stream in a clear plastic bottle. Allow the load to settle in a measuring cylinder.
2. Is it true that larger particles settle out first? How long does it take for the finer silt particles to settle?
3. How thick is each layer (in millilitres)? Make a labelled sketch of your results.
4. When the water is clear, use gentle heat from a Bunsen burner to evaporate a few drops of river water on a watch glass. **Wear safety goggles**. What do you see? What part of the river's load is this?

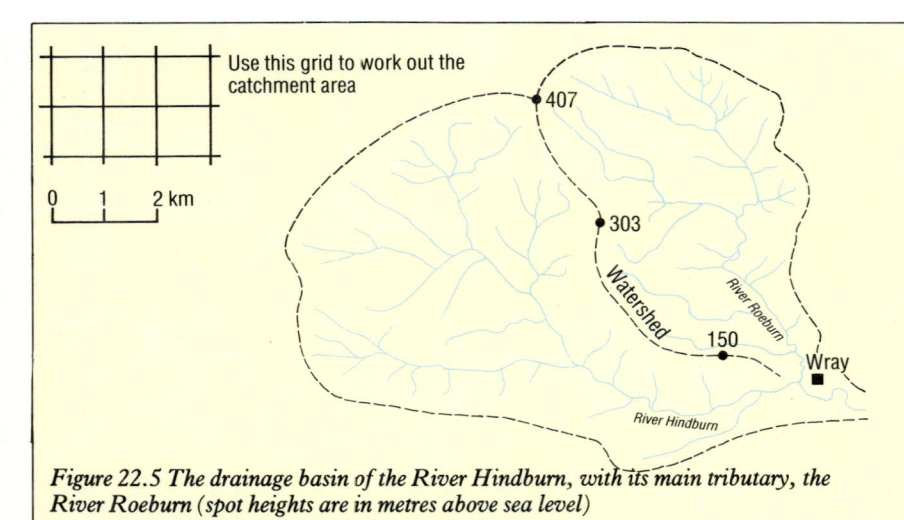

Figure 22.5 The drainage basin of the River Hindburn, with its main tributary, the River Roeburn (spot heights are in metres above sea level)

Activity 22.5

How much input?
Use tracing paper to copy the grid shown at the top of Figure 22.5.
1. What area does each square of the grid represent?
2. Overlay the grid on the map of the drainage basins. How many squares are there? What is the total area?
3. If one millimetre of rain fell, what would be the total input for the drainage basin? Your answer should be the total number of square kilometres × 1000 m^3.

What happens to the input?

Some of the water will soak into the soil and the rocks to become groundwater, and some may evaporate again. Why is there likely to be more surface run-off after many days of heavy rain?

The Wray case study

On 8 August 1967, 50 mm of rain fell in the drainage basin shown in Figure 22.5 during one hour in a thunderstorm. The water level rose quickly and the village of Wray in Lancashire was flooded. A wall of water rushed down the two river systems, carrying a mass of boulders and rubble, together with many uprooted trees. Many village houses were damaged.

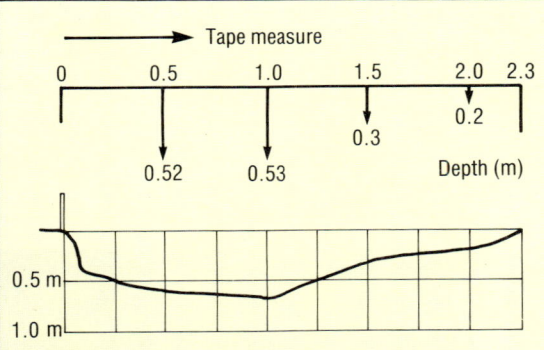

Figure 22.6 What is the discharge of this river?

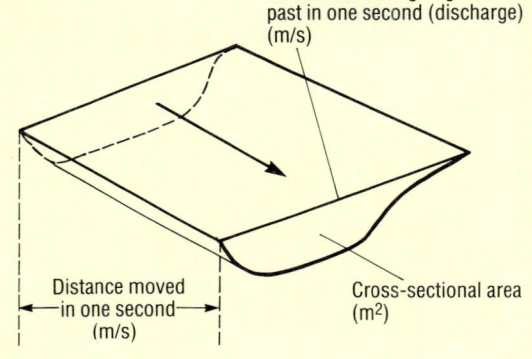

$$\text{Discharge (m}^3\text{/s)} = \text{Area of cross-section (m}^2\text{)} \times \text{Distance moved in 1 s (m/s)}$$

Figure 22.7 Calculating the discharge of a river

Summary

Rivers are able to move huge amounts of sediment and carve out their river beds. The drainage basin is a system where the water inputs are balanced by outputs. The flow processes in rivers can be measured and recorded.

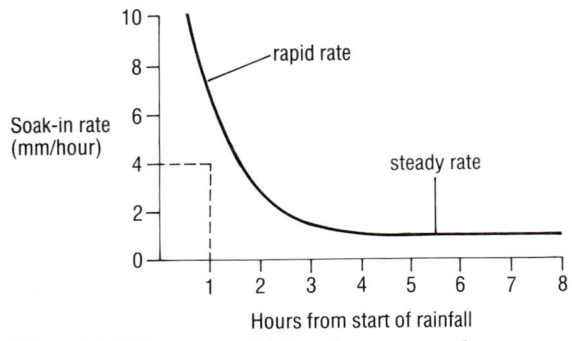

Figure 22.8 The rate at which surface water soaks away

Activity 22.6

How much output?

1. Using the method of calculation in Activity 22.5, work out the volume of the floodwater involved.
2. Look at the position of Wray shown in Figure 22.5. Why would this have been thought a good position for a settlement in the past?
3. Why is it in a potentially dangerous position?
4. Ruth Whittam was literally washed out of her house. She said, 'As water rushed in, I climbed on to the cooker but it floated away towards the window. I smashed it open with a pan and floated out.' Write a letter to Ruth explaining the disaster. Enclose a sketch map of the area to show a safer site for future building. (WP)

Activity 22.7

Measuring rivers

How fast is the flow?
Choose a stream which is shallow enough to cross easily. Mark out a 5 m length of bank. Then use a stopwatch to time how long it takes for an orange to float down between the markers. How many metres does the orange travel in one second? This is the velocity of the current.

What is the stream discharge?
The first stage is to stretch a tape measure across the stream and measure the depth every half metre as you cross (Figure 22.6). This will give you the cross-sectional area of the stream and can be drawn out on graph paper.

1. Count up the squares under the graph to find out the cross-sectional area in square metres.
2. The discharge per second is the area of the water on the cross-section multiplied by the distance it moves in one second (Figure 22.7).
3. What is the cross-sectional area of the stream shown in Figure 22.6?
4. What would be the discharge if a stream had a flow of 0.5 m/s?

Questions

1. Complete the following passage; using the words in brackets below.

   The place where a river begins is called the ..... . The network of streams flowing into each other together form a .... A small stream which joins a larger one is called a .... River valleys are usually .... shaped.

   (V, drainage basin, source, tributary)

2. Explain how a river uses pebbles to erode its bank and its bed.
3. Describe how a river transports its load.
4. Explain fully how a drainage basin works as a system.
5. Describe the circumstances that led to the flooding of Wray village in 1967
6. Study Figure 22.8. It shows the rate at which water soaked into the soil during a storm.
   a. Why is the rate so rapid in the first hour?
   b. Why does it later slow to a steady rate?

Unit 23
The atmosphere

Figure 23.1 Earth, Mercury and Venus – but which planet is which?

The Earth's mass creates enough gravitational force to hold a layer of air close to its surface – the atmosphere. Without it there would be no life and no weather. It also follows that there would be no water cycle, no breakdown of surface rocks exposed to the weather and no erosion.

Composition of the atmosphere

Air contains oxygen which animals need to breathe and carbon dioxide which is needed by plants. Air shields us from harmful radiation and stops heat escaping into space. Air is not just one gas, as shown in the table in Figure 23.2.

- Draw a pie-chart to show the data in Figure 23.2.

Ozone

This gas mainly forms when oxygen is changed by ultraviolet radiation from the Sun. Most ozone is found in the stratosphere (Figure 23.3). It blocks out most of the harmful radiation from the Sun which would otherwise scorch plants and give humans skin cancer.

Air pressure

Air has weight. A column of air weighing about one tonne is constantly pressing down on everything and everyone. We do not feel this because there is an equal pressure inside our bodies pushing outwards.

Air pressure at sea level is about 1 kg per square centimetre. The air is much thinner higher up. 18 km above the Earth's surface, the pressure is only one-tenth of that at sea-level. Find this point in Figure 23.3. Balloons carrying instruments have shown that the atmosphere has four main zones: the **troposphere**, the **stratosphere**, the **mesosphere** and the **thermosphere**.

Activity 23.1

Figure 23.1 shows three planets in our solar system – Mercury, Venus and Earth. The gravity on Mercury is about one-third that on Earth. On Venus it is nearly nine-tenths that of Earth.
1. Using the above facts, decide the name of the planet in each photo.
2. Which planet has no atmosphere? How can you tell?
3. How can you tell that two of the planets have an atmosphere?
4. Which planet has the thickest atmosphere? Say why.

Gases in air	Percentage
Nitrogen	78.09
Oxygen	20.95
Argon	0.93
Traces of other gases, including ozone, methane, carbon dioxide and water	0.03

Figure 23.2 Composition of the atmosphere

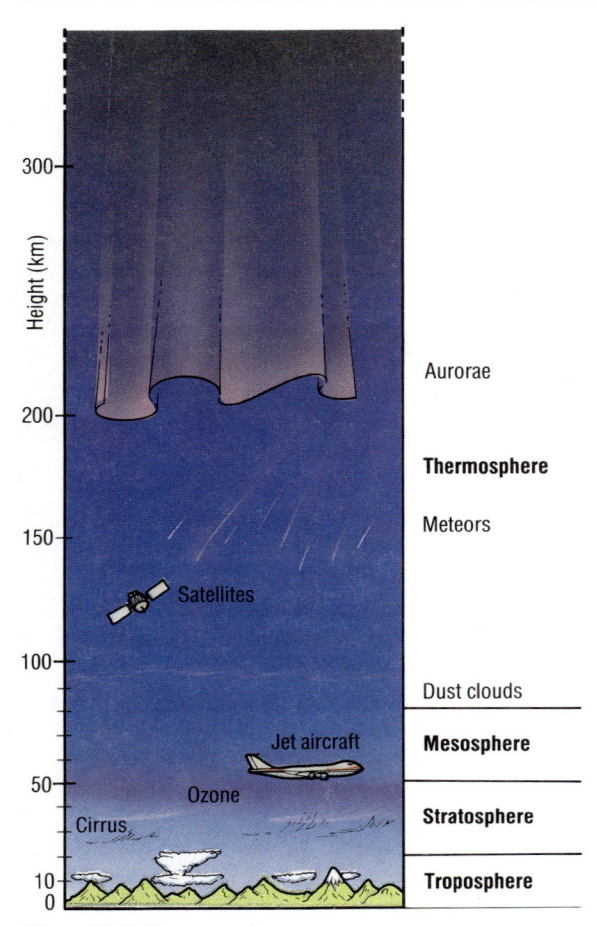

Figure 23.3 The atmosphere

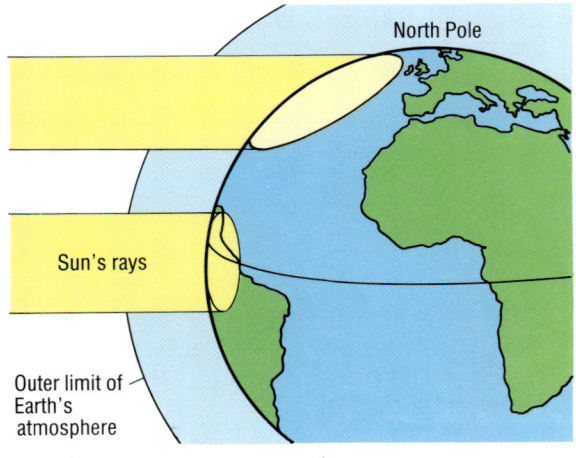

Figure 23.4 There is more solar radiation at the equator than at the poles

Activity 23.2

Air has weight
Think of a way to find out if air has weight by using a balloon and an electronic balance. Write a report explaining how you carried out this test. **WP**

Troposphere and stratosphere
This is the lowest layer of the atmosphere. It varies in thickness between 18 km over the equator and 8 km over the poles. 80% of all the air is concentrated in this layer, together with all the water vapour. All the winds, rain and weather begin in this layer. The temperature falls with height, until at the top of the troposphere it is about −55 °C.

The stratosphere rises to about 64 km above the Earth's surface. The temperature starts to rise again through the stratosphere, reaching 0 °C at a height of 50 km. The highest cirrus clouds of ice crystals are found at this level, otherwise the weather is clear.

Mesosphere and thermosphere (ionosphere)
In these final layers the air is very thin. However, there is enough air resistance in these upper layers to cause meteors to glow because of frictional heat. Radiation from the Sun causes disturbances in the thermosphere, creating the glowing curtains of light called **aurorae**. Artificial satellites orbit the Earth at heights of 120 km or above.

Controlling the Sun's heat

The atmosphere affects how much of the Sun's heat reaches the Earth's surface. The Sun's rays fall much more directly at the equator than they do at the poles, so this part of the Earth is much warmer. At the poles the rays must pass through more atmosphere and are more thinly spread, so the poles are much colder (Figure 23.4).

Activity 23.3

Find out what happens when you shine a torch at a sphere (eg a football) in a dark room. Notice how one part is lit up brightly where the light shines directly onto the ball.

Overall the atmosphere acts to filter and protect the Earth from too much sunlight during the day and keep in some of that heat at night. On the Moon where there is no atmosphere, the surface temperature rises to 100 °C at noon and drops to −150 °C by midnight.

Summary

Why does the Earth have an atmosphere? Planets that have no atmosphere have much greater surface extremes of temperature. The composition and structure of the atmosphere controls many processes from the weather to the water cycle and the erosion of rocks.

Questions

1. Why do some planets have an atmosphere when others do not?
2. What are the ways in which the atmosphere acts as 'an invisible shield' around the Earth?
3. Which layer contains all the Earth's weather?
4. At what height can you find the following: cirrus; aurorae; meteors beginning to glow; jet aircraft; artificial satellites.
5. Why are the poles so much colder than the equator?
6. What are the daily changes in temperature on the Moon's surface? Why are they so much more extreme than on the Earth?

Unit 24
Global weather

The layer of air that surrounds the Earth does not stay still. You can see evidence of this if you look outside. Branches and the leaves of trees are moving, so is smoke.

It may seem strange that air should move at all since it has weight and is pushing down on the Earth. It is the difference in temperature from place to place which gives air the energy to move – a movement we call **wind**. Strong winds are also seen on other planets. Mars has regular dust storms. The huge Red Spot on Jupiter (see Figure 27.1) is a circulating storm which has been raging for centuries in its thick atmosphere.

Convection and air circulation

When air is heated it expands. It becomes less dense, so it begins to rise. This is known as **convection**. Underneath rising air, the air is not as dense so the atmospheric pressure is *lower* than normal. As air rises, cooler heavier air sinks down to take its place and a circulating convection cell is set up. Underneath sinking air, pressure is *higher* than normal.

The global circulation

In the eighteenth century, George Hadley thought that air would rise at the equator and flow north and south to sink at the poles. He wasn't far wrong, but the distance from the equator to the poles is over 10 000 km. Air cools and sinks long before it reaches the poles. Moving air does not flow in straight lines from north to south. The Earth is spinning around its axis and the rotation deflects the moving air. This is called the Coriolis effect. It makes wind move to the right in the northern hemisphere and to the left in the southern hemisphere. This affects the way the winds move in the three convection cells and produces a pattern as shown in Figure 24.2.

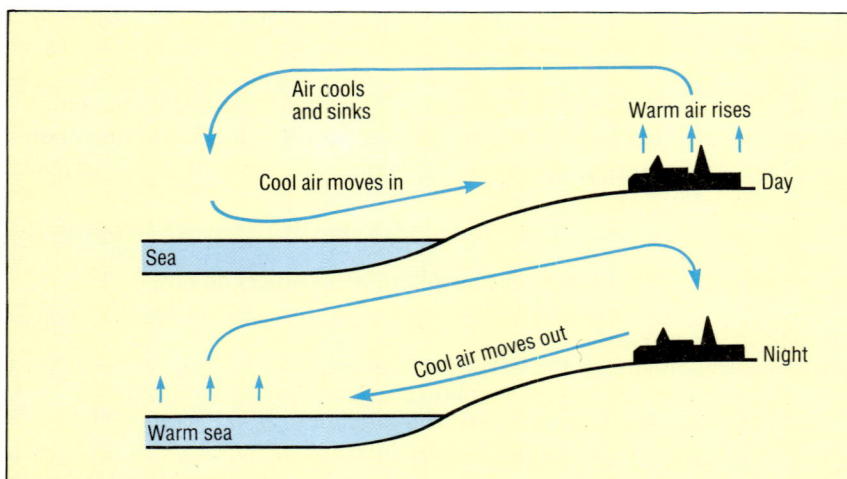

Figure 24.1 A convection cell at the seaside

Activity 24.1
How do small pieces of tissue paper move above a radiator? What is the cause of this movement?

Activity 24.2 (WP)
Discuss then write about the following question.
- What is the main cause of the differences in temperature from place to place on a planet like the Earth? (To help you, consider Figure 23.4.)

Activity 24.3
Does air expand when heated?
Stretch a rubber balloon over the end of a test tube. Gently heat the test tube. What happens?

Activity 24.4
Land and sea breezes
Figure 24.1 shows what happens at the seaside because of differences in the way the land and sea heat up and cool down.
Discuss and then write about the following questions.
1. What is happening during the day and at night? Why is it often several degrees cooler at the seaside on a hot day?
2. Write a full explanation of what is happening in both diagrams. (WP)
3. Figure 24.1 shows the circulation pattern at a local scale. What do you think the *global* pattern might be between the equator and the poles?

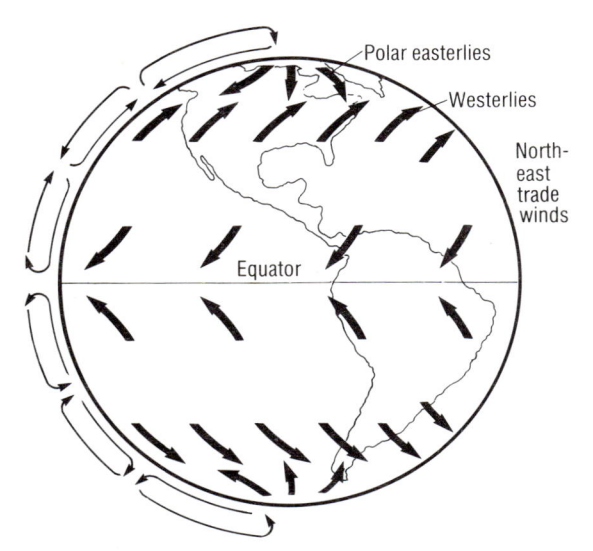

Figure 24.2 Global winds

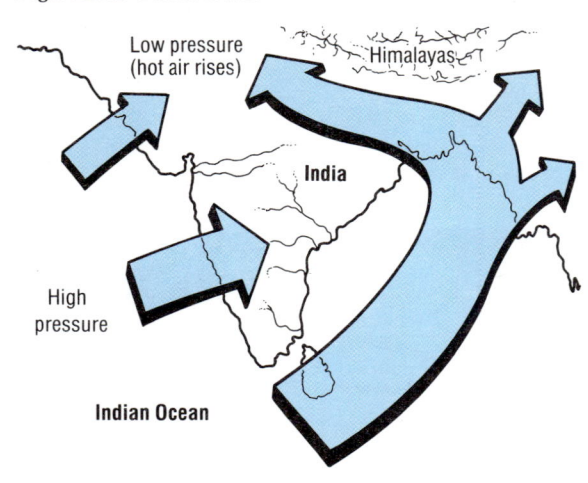

Figure 24.3 The Indian Monsoon

Activity 24.5

On the weather map
Look at Figure 24.4.
1. How many low/high pressure areas are shown?
2. Where is the pressure at its lowest/highest?
3. Make a sketch of the map, using symbols to show where the winds will be strong (S) and light (L).

Summary
Movements in the atmosphere produce the weather as winds blow from areas of high to low pressure. These movements occur right across the globe. They act to distribute the Sun's heat and produce the weather.

The effect of land and sea

Look at maps of wind circulation in a World Atlas. You will find it difficult to recognise the wind circulation patterns exactly as they are shown in Figure 24.2. This is mainly because of the uneven way in which the continents and oceans are heated. This leads to even more complications in the way the winds move. In summer, air over the continents becomes warmer than over the oceans. This happens in the Indian Monsoon (Figure 24.3). In summer, the central plains of India are heated and air rises. Low pressure develops and moist cool air from over the ocean is drawn in. This produces heavy rainfall. The opposite effect happens in winter when the sea is warmer than the land. Then the wind blows the other way and India experiences its dry season. This effect is much the same as the land and sea breezes discussed earlier but on a much bigger scale.

High and low pressure

Figure 24.4 shows a weather chart from a newspaper. The lines which circle the areas of pressure (indicated as **high** or **low**) are called **isobars**. They join together places of equal pressure (measured in millibars). The closer together the isobars, the stronger the winds. The Earth's rotation deflects the winds making them blow anticlockwise around low-pressure areas and clockwise around high-pressure areas in the northern hemisphere. The black bold lines on the map mark the positions of **fronts**, where cold and warm air meet. (These will be described more fully in Unit 25.)

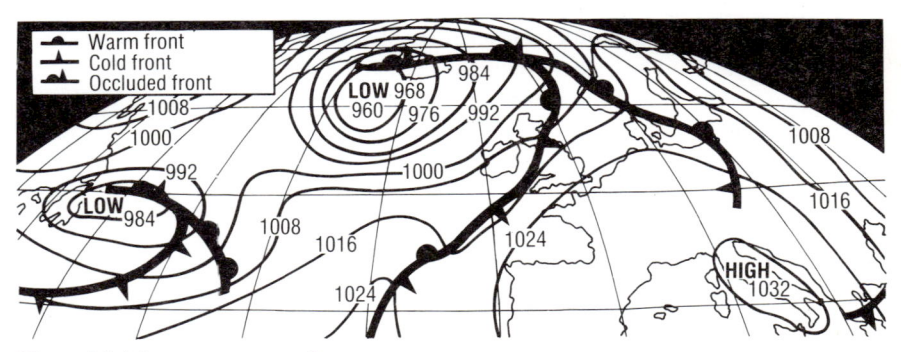

Figure 24.4 A newspaper weather map

Low-pressure areas are also called **depressions** or **cyclones**. The air in these areas is rising and cooling. Moisture condenses to form clouds and rain. High-pressure areas are called **anticyclones**. Here, the air is slowly sinking, warming and drying out. This is why high pressure produces fine dry weather in summer.

Questions
1. How do we know that air moves on other planets?
2. What is meant by a 'convection cell'?
3. How does convection help to explain global movements of air?
4. Fully explain the causes of the Monsoon.
5. What is an isobar? If isobars are close together, what does this mean?
6. Copy the following statements, choosing the correct words.

   In an anticyclone the air is sinking/rising. The pressure is high/low. Air is expanding/contracting. The air is wet/dry. The weather produced is usually fine/dull.

Unit 25
Fronts and the weather

Winds are caused by the movement of air at ground level from high to low pressure. Winds are not the only kind of weather produced. Warmer air rises within a depression, and as it does so it cools, condenses and often produces rainfall. On the other hand, sinking air in an anticyclone is warming up, so there is little condensation and cloud. Therefore there is not much rain.

Fronts

There are many situations where warm and cold air meet, to form a **front**. The British weather is often affected by warm tropical air moving north meeting cold air from the Arctic moving south. This often happens over the mid-Atlantic. The resulting storms often blow our way. They did so with great energy in the storms of early 1990. Warmer air than usual was blowing off a sea made warm by the previous hot summer. This rose up over colder polar air to form a succession of violent storms through January and February (Figure 25.1). High winds and flooding caused many deaths and damage to houses and schools. Compare the weather map (Figure 25.2) to Figure 24.4. Notice how much closer the isobars are. What does this mean? In a storm, warm air spirals up over the cold air. The slope between the two kinds of air is the line of the **warm front**. Cold air behind pushes under the warm air to form the line of the **cold front** (Figure 25.3).

Figure 25.1 Thousands of trees were blown down during the violent storms of 1990

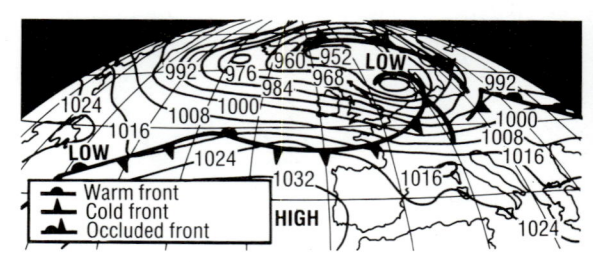

Figure 25.2 A newspaper weather map showing the storms of 1990

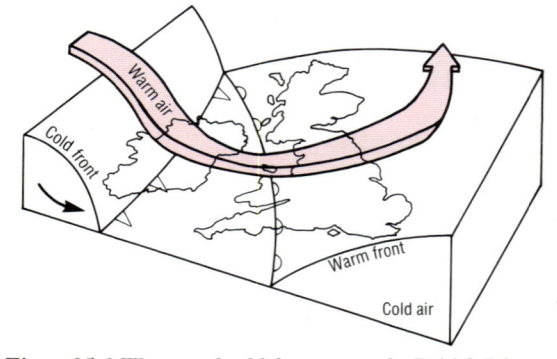

Figure 25.3 Warm and cold fronts cross the British Isles

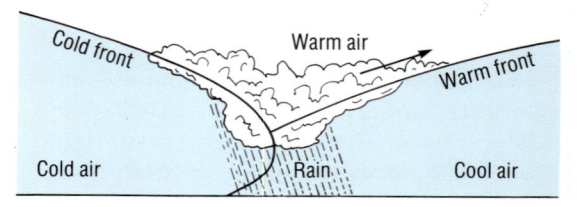

Figure 25.4 An occluded front

Activity 25.1

Write out and complete the following passage using the words in brackets below.

At a warm front, ... air rises over .... air. As it does so its temperature .... . The water vapour it is carrying ...... to form .... The rapidly rising air creates ..... pressure than normal.

(lower, warm, condenses, cold, clouds, falls)

Cold fronts and occlusions

Cold fronts form by cold air pushing under warm air. In a swirling depression, cold fronts tend to move faster than warm fronts and catch them up. Eventually the warm air is lifted up completely to form an **occluded front** (Figure 25.4).

What kind of weather?

As a depression passes over an area, there is a pattern to the weather. This is

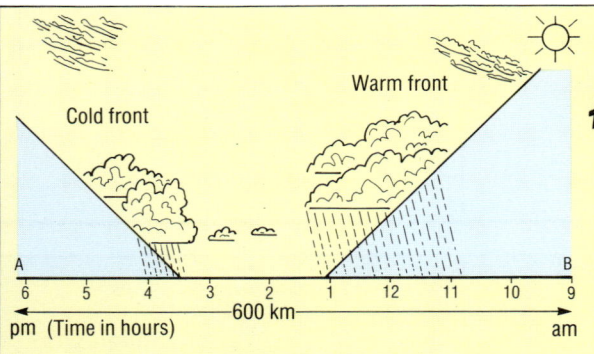

Figure 25.5 Section through a depression

Activity 25.2

Study the cross-section of a depression shown in Figure 25.5.
1 How wide is the storm from A to B?
2 How long was the interval between the cirrus cloud passing over and the first drops of rain from the warm front?
3 Imagine that you are spending a day at the beach in summer, but there is an approaching frontal system. Write an hourly log describing what the weather that you experienced was like. **WP**
4 What are the symbols used to represent the three types of front on a map?

shown in Figure 25.5. The first sign of an approaching warm front is high cirrus cloud, and the wind beginning to pick up. Then it will cloud over before it begins to rain. The temperature rises as the warm air between the fronts passes over and there is little or no rain. Then as the cold front passes over there are heavy showers.

Activity 25.4

Make a copy of the map in Figure 25.6, and use it to show a depression with its fronts moving from west to east.
1 Join the dots marking the same pressure values together to form isobars.
2 Join A to B to make a front; join B to C and B to D to make two more fronts.
3 Decide what type each front is and use the appropriate symbol to show this on the map.
4 Write the word '**LOW**' at the place where the pressure is lowest.
5 Write the words '**COLD AIR**' and '**WARM AIR**' in the correct places.
6 From what you know of the weather in a depression, describe what the weather would be like in the following places:
 • South Wales   • Edinburgh
 • Northern Ireland • London.
 • East Anglia

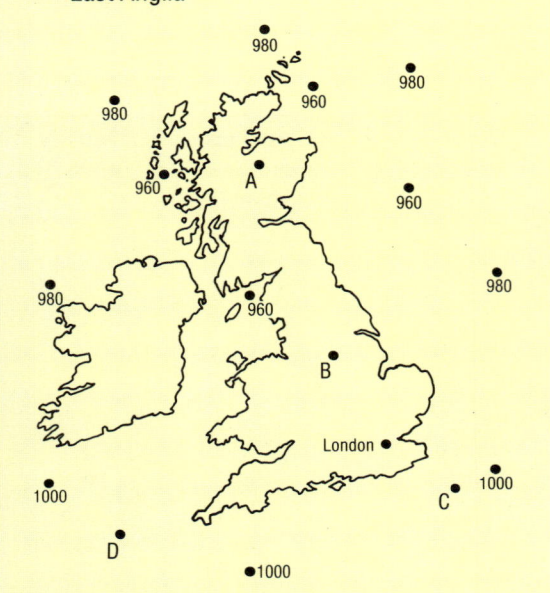

Figure 25.6 Can you work out the weather around Britain?

Activity 25.3

How much rain?

A rain gauge was used to record the amount of rainfall falling every hour as a band of rain associated with a warm front passed over. The results are shown in the table below.

Time	Rainfall (mm)
14:00 – 15:00	2
15:00 – 16:00	8
16:00 – 17:00	14
17:00 – 18:00	21
18:00 – 19:00	2
19:00 – 20:00	1
20:00 – 21:00	8
21:00 – 22:00	3

CP

1 Draw a bar graph of these results. How much rain fell in the wettest hour?
2 Label on your bar graph when the warm and the cold front passed over.

Summary

What happens when warm and cold air meet? Why were there such violent storms in early 1990? Warm air rises above cold air at a front. This causes strong winds and heavy rain.

Questions

1 Look at the map of the Northern Hemisphere in Figure 24.4 in Unit 24. Describe the possible weather in Italy, Spain, France and Britain.
2 Look at the weather forecast in the previous day's newspaper. Then write down what the weather was really like. How accurate was the forecast?
3 Use a rain gauge to make your own records of the passage of a depression.

Unit 26
The solar system

What is the solar system? How does the Earth compare to other bodies in orbit around the Sun?

Most of the stars you can see on a clear night are thousands of millions of kilometres away. Light travelling from them can take millions of years to reach us. Our Sun is just one of many stars. The **solar system** is a group of planets, including Earth, with their moons (**satellites**) all circling the Sun in paths called **orbits** (Figure 26.1). Unlike stars, planets have no natural light of their own – they can only be seen because sunlight is reflected from their surfaces. This is why we can see the Moon. The solar system also includes thousands of tiny planets called **asteroids**, as well as frozen balls of gas and dust known as **comets** and smaller rocks called **meteors**.

> 'Far out in the uncharted backwaters of the unfashionable end of the Western Spiral Arm of the Galaxy lies a small, unregarded yellow sun. Orbiting this at a distance of roughly ninety-two million miles is an utterly insignificant little blue-green planet...'
>
> Douglas Adams *Hitch-hiker's Guide to the Galaxy*

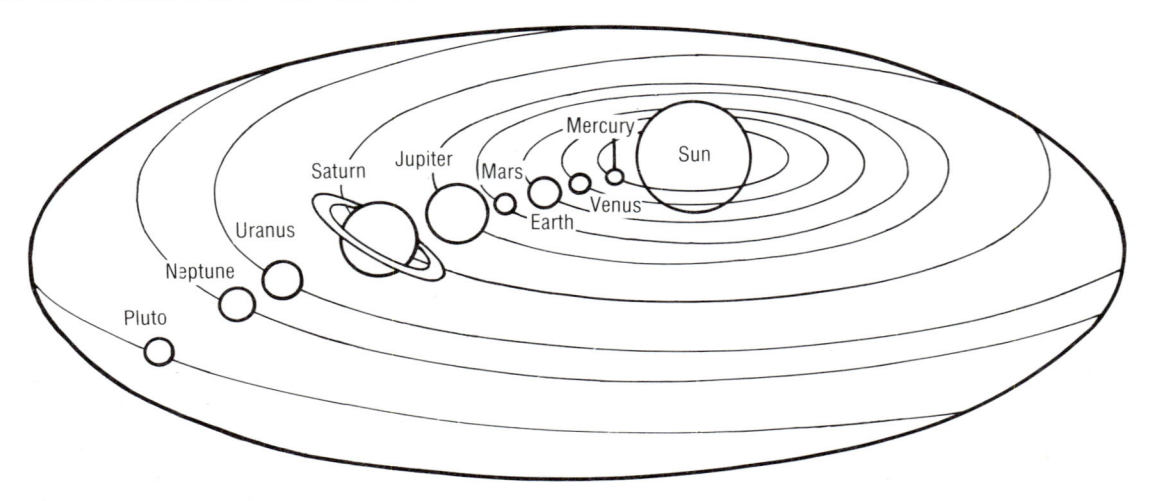

Figure 26.1 The solar system

Comparing size and densities

The different sizes of the main bodies in the solar system can be seen by comparing their diameters and densities. The diameter is the distance across each body and the density is the number of grams of material packed into each cubic centimetre.

How does the Sun control the planets?

The Earth is 150 million kilometres from the Sun. This distance is known as one **astronomical unit** (AU). Tiny Pluto is 6400 million kilometres from the Sun – 39.4 times farther away than the Earth is. Even so, it is still under the control of the Sun. Every planet rotates (spins) on its own axis and at the same time it also spins around the Sun. The time required for one complete rotation is called a day. On Earth this is 24 hours – on Jupiter it is just under 10 hours.

Body	Relative size (diameter) (Earth = 1)	Density (g/cm^3)
Sun	109.00	1.4
Mercury	0.40	5.4
Venus	0.95	5.2
Earth	1.00	5.5
Moon	0.27	3.3
Mars	0.53	4.0
Jupiter	11.18	1.3
Saturn	9.42	0.7
Uranus	3.84	1.6
Neptune	3.93	2.3
Pluto	0.31	0.4

Figure 26.2 Relative sizes and densities of the main bodies in the solar system

Activity 26.1

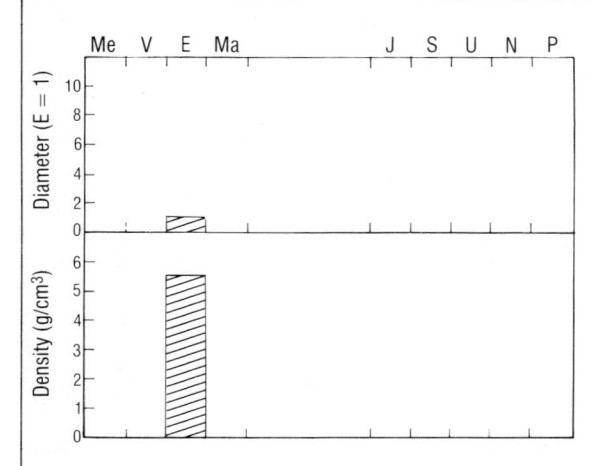

Figure 26.3 Construct a bar graph to display the information given in Figure 26.2

1. Re-arrange the list in Figure 26.2, first in order of size, second in order of density. **WP**
2. Make a copy of the bar-graph outlines as shown in Figure 26.3. Complete the two graphs. **CP**
3. The density of water is 1.00 g/cm³. Which planets have densities lower than this?
4. Which is the largest planet? Is is true that this is also the heaviest (highest density)?
5. Which are the heaviest and lightest planets, in terms of density?
6. Look carefully at the pattern of size and density. Name the planets with a *high* density but *small* diameter, and those with a *low* density but a *large* diameter. You will see that they fall into two main groups – the inner, smaller, rocky, denser planets and the outer, larger, gaseous planets. Pluto is the only exception to this because although it is of low density it is also small.

Activity 26.2

How does distance affect orbits?

The diameter of the Sun is huge compared to that of the tiny planets – so are the distances involved. You can see the relationship of distance to the period of orbit in the table in Figure 26.4.

Body	Average distance from the Sun (AU)	Period of orbit (years)
Mercury	0.4	0.2
Venus	0.7	0.6
Earth	1.0	1.0
Mars	1.5	1.9
Jupiter	5.2	11.9
Saturn	9.5	29.5
Uranus	19.2	?
Neptune	30.1	164.8
Pluto	39.4	247.7

Figure 26.4 The relationship between distance from the Sun and period of orbit of the planets in the solar system

1. Which planets have the shortest and longest periods of orbit?
2. Use these figures to make a line graph and plot distance against years **CP**
3. Use your graph to work out the period of orbit of Uranus.

Activity 26.3

The scale of the solar system

If the Sun were the size of a ball 200 mm across, then the Earth would be less than 2 mm across and 21 m away.
Cut out a disc 200 mm across from a piece of card and colour it yellow. Attach it to a ground-floor window.

1. Make scaled models of each planet using Plasticine. Mount the smaller planets on pinheads, then push each pin into the top of a stick.
2. If you have room in your school grounds, position the sticks in a line out from the model Sun, at the scaled distances as shown in the table in Figure 26.5.

Distance and scale if Sun = 200 mm diameter

Planet	Diameter (mm)	Distance (m)
Mercury	0.7	9
Venus	1.7	15
Earth	1.8	21
Mars	1.0	32
Jupiter	20.5	112
Saturn	17.2	204
Uranus	7.9	413
Neptune	7.2	643
Pluto	0.6	842

Figure 26.5 Distance of the planets from the Sun and their scale if the Sun is considered to be a ball of diameter 200 mm

3. Discuss then write. What are the most surprising facts you found out from making this model? Write a short report on your findings and say how you set up the model. **WP**

The inner planets

The smaller terrestrial planets – Mercury, Venus, Earth and Mars – are closest to the Sun. All of them have a high density – rocks and metals are found inside these planets. Only the Earth has so much water with life.

Mercury

Mercury is a small planet and its gravity is much weaker than that of the Earth. A person weighing 50 kg on Earth would weigh 19 kg on Mercury. The photo of Mercury in Figure 23.1 was taken by the Mariner 10 spaceprobe.

- What can you see that tells you Mercury has no atmosphere?
- What are the pock-marked features called and how have they formed?

There are extremes of temperature on the surface of the planet. By day it is hot enough to melt lead (up to 500 °C); by night it is cold enough to freeze oxygen (down to −200 °C).

- Why is there such a big range of temperature?

Venus

Venus is almost as big as the Earth and its gravity is about the same. See Figure 23.1.

- What is the main difference between Venus and Mercury?

For years people believed there was life on Venus but we now know this is impossible. Twenty one unmanned spacecraft have explored the planet and in 1982, Soviet Venera 14 passed through the clouds of sulphuric acid droplets to land and take the first colour television pictures of Venus. They showed a dry rocky surface. The dense atmosphere of carbon dioxide and water vapour lets in the Sun's heat but stops much of it escaping. This is called the **greenhouse effect**. The surface temperature of Venus was found to be 470 °C – how much above the boiling point of water on Earth is this?

Activity 26.6

Conditions on Venus
Place a lighted candle in a beaker and slowly tip a flaskful of carbon dioxide gas into the beaker.
1 Is carbon dioxide a light or a heavy gas? How can you tell?
2 What happens to the lighted flame? Why?

Mars

Mars is a planet half the size of Earth. Figure 26.6 shows Mars as seen by the Viking 1 spacecraft in 1976. It was taken at a distance of 322 000 km.

- What surface structures can you see?
- What is the general colour of the planet?

Activity 26.4

Conditions on Mercury
Heat a piece of lead on a tin lid over a Bunsen burner. **Wear safety goggles**. The lead will melt at a temperature of 328 °C.

- How much hotter is it on Mercury's surface during the day?

Activity 26.5 (WP)

Discuss then write about the following questions.
1 Could lead melt on Venus like it could on Mercury?
2 Will the nights on Venus be hot or very cold? Why?

Figure 26.6 Mars as seen by the approaching Viking 1 spacecraft at a distance of 322 000 km

- Do you think it likely that there is much surface water? Give reasons.
- What colour is Mars at its poles? What could cause this? It may help you to know that in the Martian northern summer the area of white shrinks in size; in winter it grows again.

In the summer of 1976, Viking 1 and 2 landed and took pictures of the surface. Figure 26.7 shows a mixture of rocks and reddish sand.

- What clues are there to the fact that there is an atmosphere?
- What Earth environment does this remind you of?

Martian scenery

The whole of Mars was photographed and apart from craters, many channels were found (Figure 26.8). They look as if they were carved by great rivers long ago, but there are no lakes or streams now. Many channels can be seen near volcanoes. They may well have been eroded by mudflows set off by melting ice below the surface. Besides valleys there are also some large canyons, formed by rift movements of the rocks. The biggest one is the Valles Marineris, 5000 km long and up to 200 km wide. Mars also has the largest volcano in the solar system called Olympus Mons. It is 25 km high and 500 km wide (Figure 26.9).

The atmosphere

The atmosphere on Mars is very much thinner than that on the Earth. It consists of 95% carbon dioxide (CO_2), 2.7% nitrogen (N_2), 0.15% oxygen (O_2) and traces of other gases including water.

There are duststorms, clouds and early morning fog, but no rain. The temperatures can rise to 10 °C on a summer's day, dropping to −100 °C at night. In winter it is much colder than this.

What about life?

The Viking spacecraft looked for evidence of life by testing air and soil samples, but they found nothing. It is possible that people might live there in the future in a domed base, but they would need spacesuits if they went outside.

Figure 26.7 A spectacular photograph of the Martian horizon taken from the Viking 2 lander

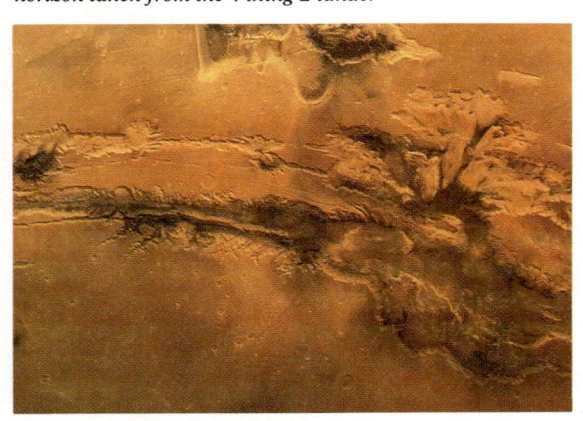

Figure 26.8 The channels on Mars were formed when volcanism melted ice beneath the surface

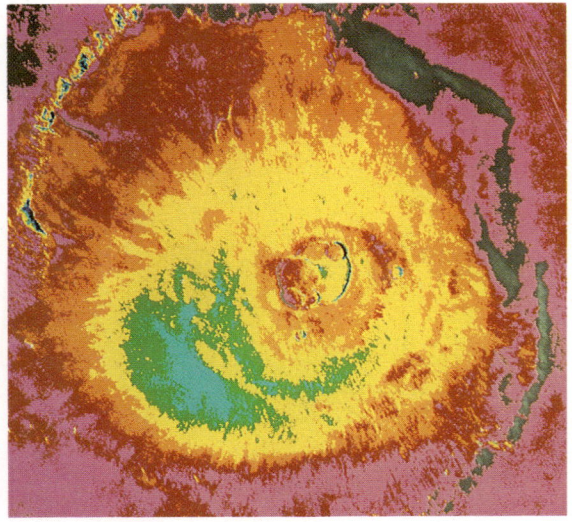

Figure 26.9 A false-colour image of the largest volcano in the solar system – Olympus Mons. The false colour reveals the differences in lava flows

Summary

The Earth is not alone in space. It is part of the solar system. Our nearest neighbours are Mercury, Venus and Mars – all very different worlds to our own.

Questions

1. Define the meaning of the following terms: solar system; orbit; satellite; asteroid; meteor; comet.
2. What are the main differences between a star and a planet?
3. What is an astronomical unit? How many AUs are there between the Sun and Pluto?
4. What is the Martian atmosphere like? Draw a pie-chart to show its composition. **CP**
5. Prepare a report on 'Conditions on the inner planets'. Then make a tape recording of your report to fit a sequence of slide photographs. **WP**

Unit 27
Discovering the outer planets

The outer planets are so far away that few details were known about them until the recent *Voyager* space probes.

Jupiter

Jupiter is the largest planet in the solar system, but its density is very low. Beneath Jupiter's thick cloudy atmosphere the planet is mainly liquid hydrogen. The banded atmosphere is in constant change. The great Red Spot (Figure 27.1) is a huge circulating storm so big it could swallow the Earth up 2.5 times. In 1978, *Voyager 1* found a thin dark ring of material around the planet and took photographs of its 16 satellites. Four of them are large enough to be visible from Earth. The 'moon' Io, has a thin atmosphere and at least nine active volcanoes erupting sulphur.

If you looked through a telescope at Jupiter you would see that it is not an exact sphere – it bulges at the equator and is flattened at the poles. This is also true of the Earth. What is the cause of this? (See Activity 27.1.)

Figure 27.1 Jupiter's Red Spot – a raging storm

Saturn

Saturn (Figure 27.3) is slightly smaller than Jupiter and is also made of frozen gases and light liquids. It is surrounded by a series of flat rings at its equator, together with 23 satellites. Saturn's density is only 0.7, less than that of water (Jupiter has a density of 1.3 and Earth has a density of 5.5).

Figure 27.3 A computer-enhanced photo of Saturn from a distance of 27 million miles. In which direction are the poles? Sketch Saturn and label the poles, the equator, the rings and the atmosphere

Photographs taken by *Voyager 1* in 1980 and *Voyager 2* in 1981 show a Red Spot smaller than Jupiter's and an east-to-west wind blowing at over 1400 km per hour. One of Saturn's satellites is called Titan. Titan is the largest satellite in the solar system and is even bigger than Mercury. It has a dense orange atmosphere of nitrogen with simple organic chemicals that might have evolved into living organisms as happened on Earth, if it were not so cold. Possible lakes of liquid methane exist on its surface.

Activity 27.1

How rotation affects shape
Make a model like the one shown in Figure 27.2, by fixing a paper ring to a spindle.
1. What happens to the shape of the paper ring as you turn the handle faster and faster?
2. On a spinning planet, where is the rotational effect the least/greatest – the pole or the equator?
3. What causes the bulge on Jupiter? Why is it greater than the Earth's bulge?

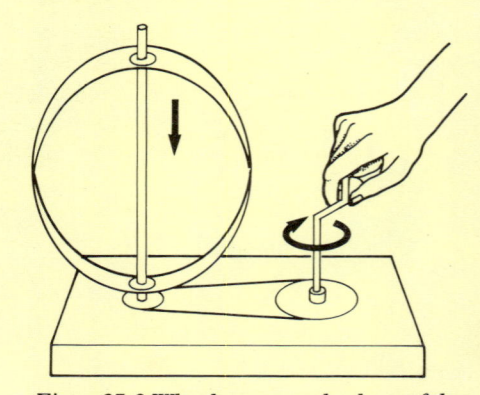

Figure 27.2 What happens to the shape of the paper ring?

Figure 27.4 Neptune

Figure 27.5 The snowy cap of Triton. The 'pink' snow is frozen nitrogen and methane

Pluto

This is a small planet with a very low density, and it is probably made of frozen methane. Pluto's orbit is not very regular and sometimes it is nearer to the Sun than Neptune. It has a satellite called Charon which was discovered in 1978. Charon is about half the size of Pluto and only 19 000 km away from it, so it is better to think of these bodies as a double planet.

Uranus

Imagine the excitement of discovering a planet no-one else has ever seen. This is what happened to William Herschel, a German musician who moved to Bath, England in 1757. His hobby was astronomy and he built his own telescope. Watching the sky in March 1781, he noticed an object with a tiny disc and thought that it was an approaching comet. As he watched it night after night for several months he realised its orbit was much more like that of a planet. His discovery caused great excitement. The new planet was called Uranus and was the first to be discovered in modern times. Its diameter is four times that of the Earth and it is similar in composition to Jupiter and Saturn. Uranus has 15 satellites. A system of rings was also discovered in 1977 and these were photographed by *Voyager 2* in 1986.

Discovery of Neptune

Some years later, it was noticed that Uranus was not moving as it should along the path of its 84-year orbit round the Sun. It was being pulled by an unknown mass, possibly another planet. John Couch Adams in England and Urbain Le Verrier in France independently worked out where this other planet might be. This was not easy to do since they did not know how massive it was nor its orbit. Before computers there was no way of quickly testing a wide variety of results. In 1846 the planet was actually seen for the first time. It was called Neptune. Neptune's orbit also showed irregularities and the existence of another planet was suspected. However, it wasn't until 1930 that Clyde Tombaugh found Pluto – the outermost planet.

New discoveries

Voyager 2 flew by Neptune in August 1989, to find a beautiful planet (Figure 27.4). High, white cirrus clouds cast their shadows on the blue clouds beneath. The dark grey spot is a huge circulating storm big enough to swallow the Earth. At least four rings were discovered. Six new moons were found, making eight in total. The most spectacular of these is Triton (Figure 27.5). It is 2720 km in diameter – slightly smaller than our Moon – and has a nitrogen atmosphere. Part of the surface is covered by pink 'snow', a frozen mixture of nitrogen and methane. The surface is extremely cold and textured by a pattern of ice ridges and grooves, with volcanoes erupting dark streaks of nitrogen through the frozen surface.

Summary

The outer planets are much farther away. Many details about them have only been learnt very recently because of the findings from successful space probes such as *Voyager 1* and *2*.

Questions

1. Draw a table to summarise the discoveries that have been made about the outer planets. Use the following headings to help you: name; size; density; distance from Sun; composition; satellites; rings; other features.
2. Name three other places in the solar system apart from the Earth and the Moon where volcanoes have been found. How do they differ from each other?
3. Why do most planets have an atmosphere while most satellites of planets do not? Name three satellites with their own atmospheres.
4. Explain why Triton has an atmosphere while our Moon does not.

Unit 28
The Sun

The Sun is our nearest star and it provides the Earth with the light and heat it needs to sustain life. Without the Sun the Earth would be a cold and desolate planet.

Looking at the Sun – Warning!!

The Sun can be studied quite easily but it is very dangerous look directly at it. The brightness can damage your eyes and the heat rays can immediately blind you. The safest way to study the Sun is to project its image onto white paper.

Activity 28.1

Effect of the Sun's heat
1. What happens to a leaf if the Sun's rays are focussed onto it using a magnifying glass? Why does this happen?
   It is thought that sunlight shining through a raindrop could set off a forest fire in a similar way.
2. Working in groups, make a list of all the facts you can think of about the Sun. Look at this list again at the end of this unit.

Activity 28.2

Making a projection box
Place a sheet of paper at one end of a shoe box. Pierce a pinhole in the other end. As light passes through the pinhole an image will be projected onto the papered end of the shoe box.
1. What do you see? If a small magnifying lens is inserted at the pinhole end, the image on the paper can be made much brighter and sharper. **Never look directly at the Sun**.
2. Try making a box like this to fit onto the end of a telescope. The instrument will focus and magnify the Sun's rays onto the paper.
3. Make a sketch of what you can see.

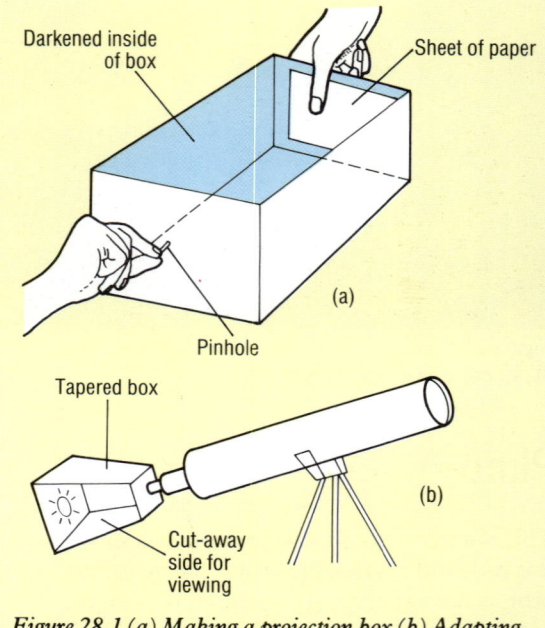

Figure 28.1 (a) Making a projection box (b) Adapting the box for use with a telescope

Sunspots

The number of spots on the Sun follows a **solar cycle** that reaches a maximum every 11 years, when the Sun is at its most active. Sunspot maximum last happened in 1991. As the Sun rotates, sunspots appear to move across its surface. Each sunspot lasts a few days or weeks and during this time it will change in size.

- How do the sunspots move? How could they be used to work out the Sun's rotation on its axis?

How big is the Sun?

The Sun is quite small compared to many other stars. It only seems bigger because it is only 143 million kilometres away. The next closest star Alpha Centauri, is 300 000 times farther away. Even so the Sun is bigger than a million Earths in volume. It is a massive ball of glowing gases, with a diameter of 1.4 million kilometres, over 100 times that of the Earth's.

Activity 28.3

Observing sunspots G
Use the method in Activity 28.1 to look for sunspots on the Sun's disc. **Never look directly at the Sun**. These are cooler areas of the Sun's surface, so they appear darker.

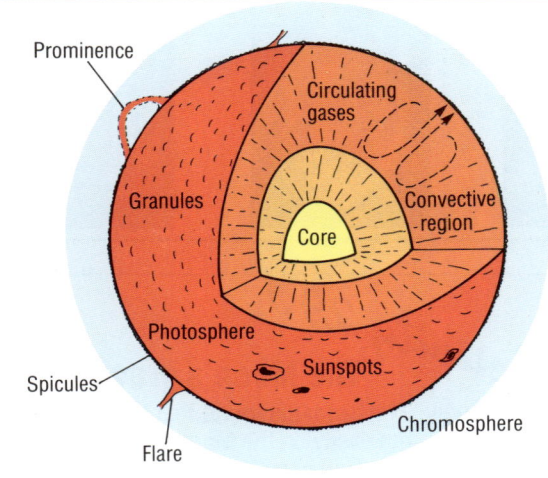

Figure 28.2 The structure of the Sun

Figure 28.3 The Sun's corona can be seen during a solar eclipse

Summary

How can the Sun be looked at safely? What is the Sun like and how long will it last? The Sun is huge compared with the Earth. It supplies the Earth with light and warmth.

Questions

1. What is the structure of the Sun? Explain how sunlight is produced.
2. Draw a pie-chart to show the Sun's gases. **CP**
3. What are sunspots? How can they be observed safely?
4. Make notes on the main features of the Sun that have been observed.
5. How is the Earth's climate affected by sunspot activity?

The Sun's structure

The densest part of the Sun is the core, where the Sun's energy is generated (see Figure 28.2). Rising currents of hot gases in the convective region form **granules** on the bright surface of the Sun – the **photosphere**. Some gas jets called **spicules** spout up to a height of about 5000 km into the outer layer of the Sun's atmosphere called the **chromosphere**, before being pulled back by the Sun's gravity. Sometimes **flares** occur near sunspots. These are eruptions of gas reaching as high as 300 000 km from the surface. A flare sends out atomic particles that cause atmospheric effects on Earth such as aurorae, and radio and computer breakdowns. Large eruptions of gases are known as **prominences**, and they follow lines of magnetic force often looping between sunspots.

When there is new sunspot activity there is more radiation into space and this can affect the Earth's climate. Air heated at the tropics will be warmer and when it meets the cold air near the poles, storms will be more vigorous.

When the Sun is eclipsed, the outer **corona** can be seen (Figure 28.3). This is made of very thin hot glowing gas, which streams out into space forming a solar wind of atomic particles.

What are conditions like?

Gases in the Sun's core are subjected to the crushing weight of millions of tonnes of material pressing down on every square centimetre. Even so, the atoms still keep their gaseous ability to move freely and to withstand the pressures caused by the Sun's own gravity. The temperature of the Sun at its surface is about 6000 °C and at the core it is about 15 million °C.

What is the Sun made of?

About 70% of the Sun is hydrogen which is the simplest and most common element in the Universe. Nearly all the rest is helium, another light and abundant gas. About 1% is made of over 70 different trace elements.

Why does the Sun shine?

As with all ordinary stars, the Sun radiates heat and light energy into space because of nuclear reactions within its core. Here, pressures due to gravity and high temperatures force the central nucleus of a hydrogen atom to fuse or combine with another hydrogen nucleus to form helium. It takes four hydrogen nuclei to form one nucleus of helium. This is known as **nuclear fusion**. The whole process causes a loss of mass and a release of energy in the form of heat and light. The intensity of the reactions and the energy released stop the Sun from collapsing under its own gravity.

How long will the Sun last?

Every second, 600 million tonnes of hydrogen is turned into helium and 4 million tonnes of the Sun's mass is lost. Eventually the Sun will use up all its hydrogen and the nuclear reactions that produce sunlight will stop. However this will not happen for at least another 5000 million years.

Unit 29
The Moon

Figure 29.1

Where is the Moon?

The Moon is the Earth's natural satellite, orbiting at an average distance of 384 000 km – 9.5 times the distance around the Earth's equator. It is a sphere of rock 3476 km in diameter, about the same as the distance across Australia from north to south.

What are surface conditions like?

The Moon has no atmosphere nor surface water. The days are very hot and the nights are intensely cold. The density of the Moon is only 3.34 compared to the Earth's 5.5. This means that the Moon's gravity is only one-sixth that of the Earth. For any pull of gravity to a body there is an **escape velocity**. The escape velocity of the Moon is 2.37 km/s and an object must move faster than this to avoid being pulled back by the Moon's gravity. There isn't an atmosphere because gases are able to move much faster than this and have been lost into space. By contrast, the Earth's escape velocity is 11.18 km/s which is enough to keep an atmosphere. This is the rate a rocket has to go to avoid being pulled back by the Earth's gravity.

The Moon's brightness

At night, when it is a full Moon, it is bright enough for you to be able to read this book. The changing shape of the Moon seen in the Moon's 'phases' is caused by its orbit and the fact that it has no light of its own. Surprisingly the surface is dark, reflecting only 7% of the light from the Sun. It seems bright to us because it is so near.

The Moon's surface

The surface is pitted with craters and covered with loose dust produced from the impact of meteorites over millions of years. In many places the dust forms a layer called **regolith**, the lunar soil. The Apollo astronauts found that all moonrock is igneous, which means that it has formed from cooling magma. There are no active volcanoes now, but the darker areas of the Moon's surface called **maria** are low-level plains of basaltic lava. The lighter coloured highlands are older and more rugged.

Phases of the Moon

The Moon orbits the Earth once every 27 days, 7 hours and 10 minutes. All that time one half of the Moon is in sunlight but the angle that the Moon makes with the Earth changes. This alters the amount of the Moon's surface that we can see from the Earth. These changes are called phases (see Figure 29.1).

Activity 29.1
The Moon's gravity

The Apollo 11 astronauts found that they could walk and jump easily on the Moon's surface in their spacesuits and heavy backpacks.
1. Do ten press-ups against a wall (see Figure 29.2). This requires about the same effort as doing ten press-ups in the Moon's gravity. Use a stopwatch to measure your pulse rate.
2. After resting, do ten press-ups from the floor against the Earth's gravity. Measure your pulse rate again.
3. How does each activity affect your pulse rate?
4. Draw three bar graphs of your pulse rate:
   a at rest,
   b after the 'wall' press-ups,
   c after the floor press-ups.
   Explain these results. **CP**

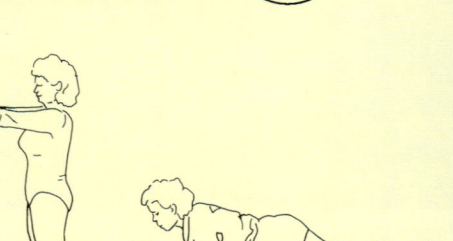

Figure 29.2 Comparing the Earth's gravity to that of the Moon

Activity 29.2
Looking at the Moon

Unlike the Sun, it is safe to look directly at the Moon. You will easily see the darker maria and the lighter mountainous areas. Binoculars or a telescope will reveal much more detail – you will be able to see the Moon's craters and the rays of dust thrown out from them.

- Watch the Moon each night through its cycle of phases over 27 days. Sketch its shape and any features you see each night. Do you see the same shapes as you saw in the model activity?

Figure 29.3 The phases of the Moon

Activity 29.3

The Moon's phases

Make a model Moon from an old tennis ball. Paint one half white – to represent the Moon's day – and the other half black. Put it on a table with the white half facing towards the light from a window (the Sun). Position yourself with the model 'Moon' between you and the window, so that your eyes are at the same level as the ball. Your eyes are the view from Earth. How much of the white area (the Moon's day) can you see?

1 Move the model through the positions shown in Figure 29.3 and sketch how much of the Moon's white disc you can see in each position.
2 Compare your finished sketches with the phases in Figure 29.1.

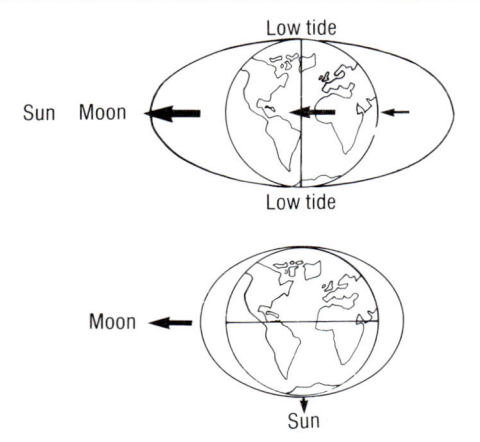

Figure 29.4 (a) Spring tides. Why is the tidal bulge on both sides of the Earth? (b) Neap tides. Why are these tides smaller?

Tides

Have you ever wondered what causes the oceans of the Earth to rise and fall? The Moon's gravity pulls the oceans towards it on the side facing the Moon. The solid Earth is also pulled slightly, away from the waters on the side farthest away from the Moon, to make the second bulge (see Figure 29.4). The arrows show the relative amounts of movement. As the Earth rotates, both high tides sweep around the world every 24 hours. Although the Sun is bigger than the Moon it is farther away, so the effect of its gravity is not as great. When the Sun, Moon and Earth are in a line their combined gravitational pull causes extra high tides called **spring tides** (Figure 29.4(a)). When the Sun and Moon pull at right angles to each other the Sun's gravity weakens the effect and causes the smaller **neap tides** (Figure 29.4(b)).

Summary

The Moon affects us every day as it causes the Earth's tides. Unlike the Earth, it is a dry lifeless planet with no atmosphere.

Questions

Read the *Daily Echo* report and then answer the questions below.
1 Why are there future plans to study the Moon?
2 Write a report to NASA explaining the advantages of a lunar base. Advise them of how long people should spend at the base. **WP**

Daily Echo

Search for the Moon's secret water

The Americans plan to use a satellite probe to look for ice in craters near the Moon's poles in the 1990s. If ice exists, it would be easier to set up a manned lunar base. As well as providing water, hydrogen could be extracted for rocket fuel. The Moon could be used as a base for exploring the solar system. Rockets would need little fuel and could be launched more cheaply than from Earth.

Unit 30
The universe

Astronomy began when people made discoveries about movements in the sky. Ancient peoples used the Sun and the Moon to measure time and the seasons. Long before 2500 BC calendars based on the Moon were in use. People began to think of ideas about the origin of the universe.

Different beliefs

The Sun is vital to all life on Earth and this was recognised by most ancient peoples who worshipped it as a god. The Aztecs, Incas and Mayas of the Americas all worshipped the Sun, so did the ancient Egyptians. They noticed that the River Nile flooded every year soon after the star Sirius appeared. They used this event to mark the start of their farming year.

The geocentric (Earth-centred) theory
The Greeks were the first people to suspect that the Earth was a globe, but they thought that the Earth was fixed at the centre of the universe (Figure 30.1(a)). They believed the stars, Sun and planets went around the Earth. This idea lasted for about 1300 years.

The heliocentric (Sun-centred) theory
In 1543 Nicholas Copernicus realised that the Earth was just an ordinary planet orbiting the central Sun, along with the other planets of the solar system (Figure 30.1(b)). It took a long time for people to accept that this was the truth.

Figure 30.1 These two diagrams show two different ideas about the solar system. What are the main differences?

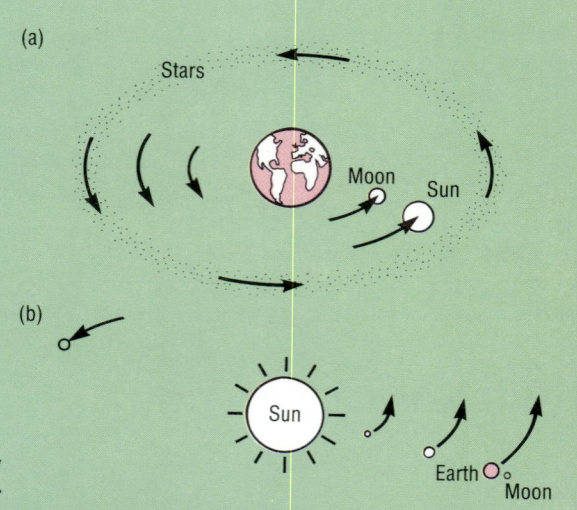

What lies beyond the solar system?

Beyond the farthest planet Pluto are the stars – huge shining balls of gas like our Sun. They look like tiny lights because they are so far away. The unaided eye can see about 6000 stars. Many more can be seen with binoculars or a simple telescope. Astronomers with large telescopes can see countless millions of stars scattered throughout space.

What is a light year?

A light year is the distance light travels in one year – 9.5 million million km. The nearest star to the Sun, Proxima Centauri, is 4.3 light years away. The nearest and brightest star seen in the northern hemisphere is Sirius.

What is a galaxy?

A galaxy is dust, gas and millions of stars held together by the force of gravity. Our Sun is one of at least 100 000 million stars that make up our galaxy, called the **Milky Way**. This is a huge spiral group of stars, slowly circulating around the central hub. The Sun and its planets take 225 million

Figure 30.2 Galaxy M31 in Andromeda. There are possibly 100 000 million stars in this whirlpool of stars

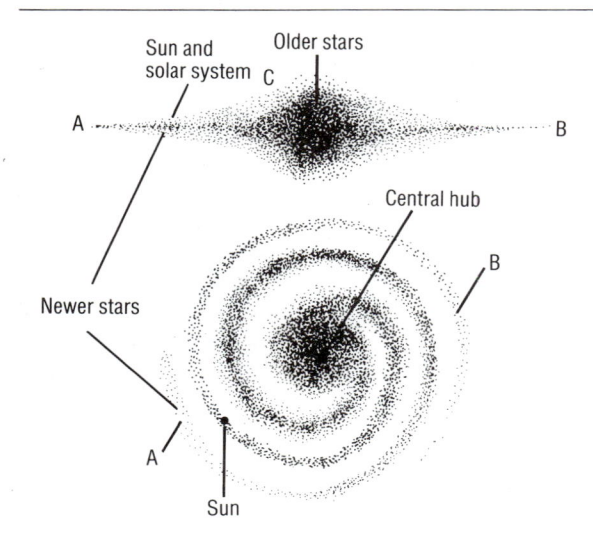

Figure 30.3 Plan and section of our galaxy. How long would it take to cross from A to B at the speed of light; and from C to D

Activity 30.2 (CP)

1. Look at Figure 30.3. If the distance A–B across the spiral is about 100 000 light years, then roughly how thick is the galaxy as seen side on?
2. Use the figures in the table below to make a scaled diagram of some of the stars closest to us:

Star	Number of light years away from Earth
Proxima Centauri	4.3
Barnard's	5.9
Sirius	8.8
61 Cygni	11.2
Procyon	11.4
Van Maanen's	13.9
Altair	16.6

Figure 30.4 The Virgo cluster is the nearest cluster after the Local Group with over 2500 galaxies – 72 million light years away

years to go around once. Figure 30.2 shows what the Milky Way might look like. It is a photo of Andromeda, 2.2 million light years away from us. The diagram in Figure 30.3, shows the position of our Sun on one of the spirals.

Activity 30.1

1. How did early astronomy begin?
2. What did ancient civilisations use as a basis for their calendars?
3. Why was the Sun regarded as so important by so many early cultures?
4. How did the ancient Egyptians know when the River Nile was going to flood?
5. What is the geocentric theory? How did it differ from the heliocentric theory?
6. What is a light year? Does it measure time or distance? Why is this measurement needed?

Other galaxies

The table in Activity 30.2 shows just a few of the stars in the Milky Way. People using large telescopes can see millions of similar galaxies in all directions in space. The universe may contain 100 000 million galaxies, each one with about the same number of stars as the Milky Way. Most galaxies belong to groups called **clusters**. Figure 30.4 shows the Virgo cluster. The Milky Way is part of a small cluster of 20 galaxies known as the **Local Group**. Beyond the Local Group are thousands of larger clusters – many containing over 1000 galaxies.

What makes stars shine?

Like the Sun, stars produce their own light by nuclear fusion reactions. If you use a simple telescope to look at the stars you will see that they are slightly different colours. This is caused by different surface temperatures. The hottest stars are blue-white at over 10 000 °C. Medium-hot stars like our Sun are yellow at 6000 °C. The coolest stars are red, at 2000 °C.

How do stars change?

Stars are born, then they mature, grow old and die. In space there are huge swirling clouds of gas and dust called **nebulae**. Study of them has led to the **Nebula theory** which explains the origin of the solar system and how stars form. This theory is discussed below.

Birth

It is possible to see new stars forming in nebulae. It is reasonable to assume that millions of years ago the Sun also began its life in the same way. Within the swirling nebula, some material forms separate clumps as different particles collide. Then these clumps collide and combine. Their gravitational mass attracts other material to them. Eventually a giant ball is formed. This slowly collapses and shrinks, as material presses in towards the centre. The central core heats up as particles of material are forced more closely together by the inward pull of gravity. These collapse and heating takes place over millions of years.

The beginning of sun/starlight
When a temperature of 10 million °C is reached in the core, hydrogen gas starts turning to helium as the nuclear-fusion reactions begin. Energy is released and the star shines. The shrinking process discussed above stops when the outward pressure of hot gases balances the inward pull of gravity. Our Sun was born like this 5000 million years ago, and is now about half way through its life cycle. Clumps of matter in the outer nebula surrounding the central Sun became the planets.

How do stars die?
A star dies when all the hydrogen is used up. The star's core then heats up and begins to expand to become a **giant**. Its surface cools and it starts to glow red. In 5000 million years time this will happen to the Sun. It will then grow so large it will swallow up Mercury, Venus, Earth and Mars. Eventually most stars collapse to leave an outer layer of expanded gases as a nebula. The collapsing core becomes a superdense star called a **white dwarf**, about the size of the Earth. Finally the white dwarf gives off its last light and becomes a cold black dwarf.

Supernovae
Sometimes big stars end their lives in a sudden explosion. In just a few hours the star increases in brightness to the brilliance of millions of suns. The explosion blows away most of its material into space. These are rare events and only four have ever been observed in our galaxy. After its death a supernova may leave a dense neutron star (Figure 30.5). This can continue to collapse to form a tiny superdense star called a **black hole**. The gravity of black holes is so strong that nothing, not even light, can escape from them.

Figure 30.5 The crab nebula – all that is left of a supernova explosion. At its centre is a neutron star

Activity 30.3
1. Explain what a galaxy is.
2. What is the name of galaxy of which our Sun is a member?
3. What is meant by a cluster? How many galaxies are there in our local cluster?
4. What are the surface temperatures of the following types of star: yellow; blue-white; red?
5. What is a nebula?
6. When a star is born, what force makes the centre of the star heat up? Why is this?
7. What causes a star to die?
8. What is a supernova?
9. Why is a black hole so called?

How did the universe begin?

This is a much bigger question than just asking how the Sun and the Earth began, and one that people have asked for hundreds of years.

Early beliefs
In ancient times people believed that gods and goddesses were in control of the universe they had created. The Greeks thought that the universe was once a motionless mixture which later became a whirling mass. Cold matter fell out of this to make the Earth. Later the Sun and the planets came from the Earth.

Religious beliefs
Both the Moslem and Christian faiths explain the universe in terms of a single creator, God. The Bible begins with the words 'In the Beginning God created the heaven and the earth ... without form ... empty ... dark ... then God said 'Let there be light.'

An old Indian Hindu belief is that the universe is born, then over a long time it is destroyed and remade in a cycle (Figure 30.6). This is interesting because it fits with some modern ideas about how the universe changes.

The expanding universe
In the late 1920s Edwin Hubble discovered that not only were there hundreds of millions of galaxies, but that they are all moving away from each other at a steady rate. He concluded that the universe must be expanding.

Figure 30.6 The Hindu god Shiva controls the cycle of creation, destruction and rebirth

Activity 30.4

Partly inflate a balloon and draw tiny galaxy shapes close together on the balloon with a biro. Inflate the balloon. What happens to the 'galaxies'?

The big bang theory

What is causing the universe to expand and the galaxies to move away from each other? Georges Lemaitre proposed that at one time the universe was a compressed, superdense blob of matter that exploded. That explosion termed the 'big bang' was the origin of the universe. According to measurements of rates of expansion, this explosion must have happened between 10 000 and 20 000 million years ago. Matter has been flying apart ever since. Will the universe expand for ever? It is possible that gravity could cause the galaxies to slow down and fall back together to become another superdense blob of matter. This is rather like a ball being thrown into the air. It eventually stops moving away from the Earth and then falls back again.

An oscillating universe?

If this happens, the universe could be first expanding, and then shrinking to another big bang in a cycle of creation and destruction.

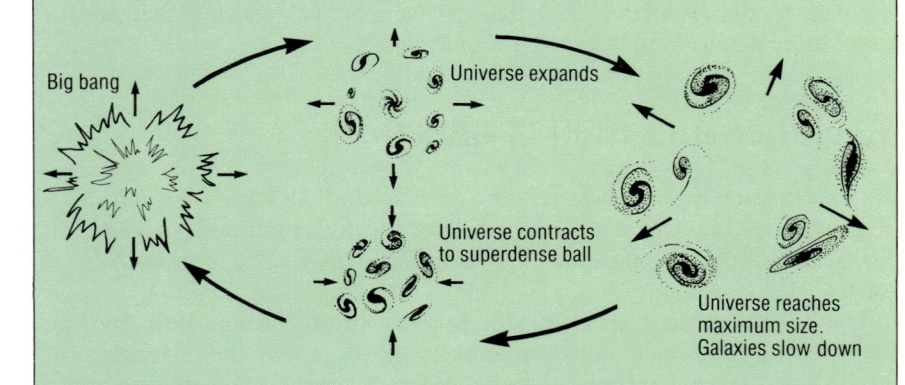

Figure 30.7 The cycle in an oscillating universe. What does 'oscillating' mean?

Summary

The sheer size of the universe is difficult to imagine. Scientists are still finding distant objects at the limit of the observed universe. Over the centuries there have been many ideas that people have had about the origin of the universe. It is interesting to compare these with what most scientists believe now.

Questions

1. How accurate are the beliefs of the Ancient Greeks, compared to the Nebular Theory?
2. How close is the biblical account of creation to today's theories?
3. How close is the theory of an oscillating universe to the Hindu belief of creation?
4. Find out what your friends think about the beginning of the universe by preparing a questionnaire. **WP** **CP**
   Make graphs of your results.
   Write a report on your conclusions.
5. Find out more about distant galaxies and deep space from books in your local library.

Unit 31
Exploring space

How can exploring the Sun, Moon, planets and stars help us to understand many of the processes that happen on Earth? The effects of tides, day and night, months, seasons and the year are all caused by other objects in space.

History of exploration

Although people have long studied the stars and planets, it wasn't until astronomers like William Herschel began using better telescopes that we learnt more detail about distant stars and galaxies.

Machines and men in space

In 1957, the first machine was put into orbit around the Earth – *Sputnik 1* (Figure 31.1). This was achieved by making a rocket engine able to fly at 40 000 km/h – the velocity needed for an object to escape from the Earth's gravity.

The first astronaut in space was the Russian Yuri Gagarin in 1961. By July 1969 the Americans had landed two men on the Moon – Neil Armstrong and Buzz Aldrin. Since that time, all of the planets in the solar system have been explored apart from Pluto, using different unmanned robot spaceprobes controlled by on-board computers and by commands sent from Earth.

Voyagers 1 and 2

These two spaceprobes were launched in 1977 and have sent back much new information about Jupiter, Saturn, Uranus and Neptune and their rings and moons. *Voyager 1* left the solar system after its encounter with Saturn but *Voyager 2* went on from Saturn to reach Uranus. This spaceprobe has travelled 33 AU in just over 8.5 years.

Voyager 2 went on to reach Neptune in August 1989, where it took many spectacular photographs of the blue planet and its moons.

Where is *Voyager 2* now?

Voyager 2 and its twin *Voyager 1* are well on their way out of the solar system. They will both continue to transmit signals until the year 2014. Even though *Voyager 2* is travelling at 69 567 km/h, it will not come within one light year of another star for the next 958 000 years. There is a remote chance that life somewhere else in the universe might find the craft so they each have on board a copper disc entitled *The Sounds of Earth* with messages of peace.

In spite of the huge distances involved, the control team got the best possible results from *Voyager 2* at Neptune. One problem was the time delay. It took messages 4 hours 6 minutes to reach *Voyager* from Earth.

Figure 31.1 **Sputnik 1** – *the first satellite to orbit the Earth. It weighed 83.6 kg and measured 58 cm across*

Activity 31.1
1 What is an AU and what distance did *Voyager 2* cover in millions of kilometres?
2 Roughly how far did the spacecraft travel in one year? In what year did it reach Uranus?

Activity 31.2
Swing a conker round and round on the end of a piece of string.
1 When you let go what happens to the conker?
2 Explain how this compares with what happens to *Voyager* as it goes past a planet.

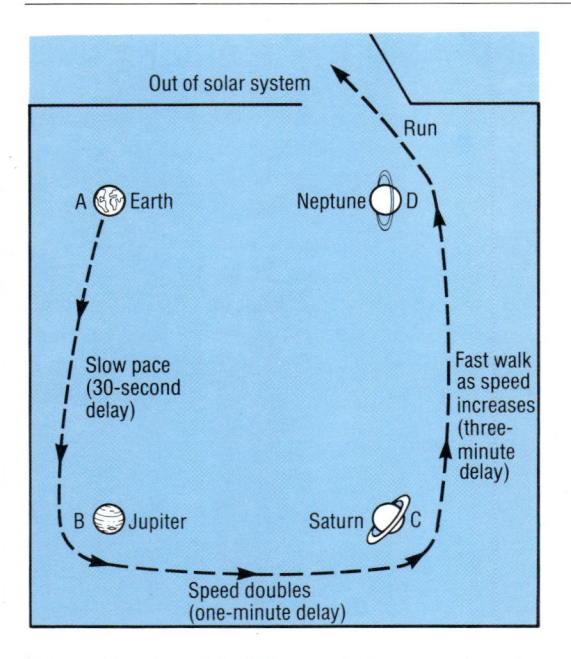

Figure 31.3 A model of Voyager's journey, where the classroom represents part of the solar system.

Activity 31.3

Problems of remote control

Make out a plan similar to the one shown in Figure 31.3. The points A, B, C and D represent planets. They could be set out round your classroom. Ask a friend to act as *Voyager*.

The journey from Earth (A) to Jupiter (B) is made by placing one foot slowly in front of another. At B, *Voyager* doubles its speed – your friend can now walk slowly. If any change in direction is needed now you must give a command like 'three paces to the left' but your friend must not react to this command for a minute. As *Voyager* comes around planet C (Saturn) its speed doubles again but now you must allow for a 1.5 minute delay in your commands reaching *Voyager*. Finally between Uranus and Neptune the delay is 3 minutes. Imagine having to do this if the delay in response was over 4 hours! Try to guide your 'spacecraft' without crashing.

Questions

1. List five processes on Earth caused by other bodies in space.
2. Describe three different ways in which the solar system has been explored. **WP**
3. What is the 'slingshot effect'?
4. Design a newspaper front page reporting on *Voyager's* encounter with aliens in 2015. **DTP**

The Daily Echo   26 August 1989

Fantastic voyager's incredible light show

For the past 12 years *Voyager 2* has been hurtling through space to the edge of the solar system. It has travelled 7.2 thousand million km at the rate of 1.6 million km a day and reached Neptune just one second late. Voyager is a 1 tonne spaceship no bigger than a car (Figure 31.2). It has TV cameras on board and other devices such as a magnetometer to measure magnetic fields around planets. Yet in many ways the spacecraft is quite primitive – its computer is not even as powerful as many of today's lap computers. Even so, pictures revealed frozen lakes and volcanoes erupting nitrogen on the surface of Triton, Neptune's moon. Cirrus clouds were seen in Neptune's atmosphere and rings were discovered.

How it got there

To increase velocity, scientists were able to take advantage of a line-up of planets that happen once every 176 years. Every time the craft soared past a planet it 'stole' some of the energy from the gravitational field in what is called the **slingshot effect**. The idea of using this effect first came from a research student Gary Flandros, who noticed the way in which comets speed up as they pass near planets.

Figure 31.2 Voyager's journey into space. Voyager 1 = orange track; Voyager 2 = red track

Summary

Most of what we know about the solar system has come from the findings of robot spacecraft in the last 20 years. Nearly all the information about the outer planets comes from just two spacecraft, *Voyager 1* and *Voyager 2*.

Glossary

ALLOY	A mixture of two or more metals.
ANTICLINE	An upfold in rock layers.
ASH	Powdered rock produced by volcanic explosions.
ASTEROID	A small planet or large rock in orbit around the Sun.
ASTRONOMICAL UNIT	One unit is the average distance between the Earth and the Sun – 150 million kilometres.
ASTRONOMY	The study of space and the heavenly bodies.
ATMOSPHERE	The layer of gases surrounding the Earth and many other heavenly bodies including the Sun.
AQUIFER	A permeable layer of rock acting as an underground water reservoir.
AUREOLE	An area of rocks metamorphosed by heat surrounding an igneous intrusion.
AURORA	A curtain of shimmering lights in the night sky caused by charged particles from the Sun being trapped by the Earth's magnetic field.
BASALT	The most common lava on the Earth's surface.
BATHYLITH	A large intrusion where magma has cooled slowly underground.
BAUXITE	The only workable mineral ore of aluminium.
BIG BANG	The name given to a possible explosion of energy and formation of matter when the universe began.
BLACK HOLE	A collapsed star that is so dense, its gravity will not allow its own light to escape.
BLOCK MOUNTAINS	Mountains formed by earth movements along vertical faults.
CASSITERITE	A mineral ore of tin.
CERRUSITE	A mineral ore of lead.
CIRRUS	Thin high-level wispy cloud.
CLUSTER	A group of neighbouring galaxies.
COMET	A heavenly body of dust and gases with a long tail in an elliptical orbit around the Sun.
CONFLUENCE	The place where two streams meet and flow together.
CONTINENT	A thicker section of the Earth's crust partly above sea level.
CONTINENTAL DRIFT	The sideways movement of the continents.
CONTINENTAL SHELF	Area of shallow sea-floor on the edge of continents.
CORE	The denser central part of a star or planet.
CORIOLIS EFFECT	The deflection of winds caused by the Earth's rotation.

CORONA	The glowing ring of gases of the Sun's atmosphere, seen in an eclipse.
CRUST	The thin, rigid outer layer of the Earth.
DELTA	A triangular shaped deposit found at the mouths of some rivers.
DENSITY	The mass of material packed into one cubic centimetre.
DIAMOND	The hardest known mineral, value 10 on Mohs' scale.
DISCHARGE	The volume output of a stream in cubic metres.
DOLERITE	A medium-grained basaltic type rock found in dykes and sills.
DRAINAGE BASIN	The area drained by a river and its tributaries.
DYKE	An igneous intrusion which cuts across the grain of the rock layers.
EARTHQUAKE	The shaking of the Earth caused by sudden rock movements.
EPICENTRE	The nearest point at the surface to the focus of an earthquake.
EROSION	The wearing away of the land surface by water, ice, wind and movements caused by gravity.
ESCAPE VELOCITY	The speed at which an object must travel into space to avoid being pulled back to the surface of a planet.
ESTUARY	The funnel-shaped mouth of a river.
EVAPORITE	A salt rock deposited in arid conditions as water evaporates.
EXFOLIATION	The peeling away of outer rock layers in weathering.
FAULT	A crack in the rocks along which there is movement.
FISSURE	An open crack in the rocks caused by tension.
FLARE	An upward stream of very hot gas from the Sun's surface.
FOCUS	Underground location of a rock movement that causes an earthquake.
FOLD MOUNTAINS	A range of mountains formed by crumpling of rock layers.
FRONT	The boundary between warm and cold air.
FUSION (NUCLEAR)	The formation of helium from hydrogen under intense heat and pressure, so releasing energy.
GALAXY	A large circulating spiral system consisting of millions of stars.
GEOCENTRIC THEORY	The idea that the Earth is at the centre of the universe.
GEYSER	A fountain of superheated water and steam.
GNEISS	A light and dark banded metamorphic rock formed at high pressures and temperatures.
GRANULES	The mottling of the Sun's surface due to gas convection.

GRAPHITE	A soft mineral of carbon.
GRAVIMETRIC SURVEY	Measurement of gravity differences.
GRAVITY	The force of attraction between heavenly bodies.
GREENHOUSE EFFECT	The heavier gases such as carbon dioxide which trap the Sun's heat and prevent heat loss into space.
GROUNDWATER	Water held in the rocks below ground.
GULF STREAM	A warm ocean current which flows from the Gulf of Mexico to Northern Europe, also called the North Atlantic Drift.
HAEMATITE	An iron ore mineral.
HELIOCENTRIC THEORY	The idea that the Sun is at the centre of the solar system.
HORNFELS	Slaty rock formed mainly by heat changes in contact metamorphism.
HORST	A block mountain formed by fault movements.
HYDROLOGICAL CYCLE	The water cycle.
IGNEOUS	Rock formed from cooling of molten magma or lava.
INDEX FOSSIL	A distinctive fossil used to identify and date a rock layer.
INTRUSION	A body of magma which pushes its way into surrounding rocks.
ISLAND ARC	A chain of islands formed above a subducting plate.
ISOBAR	A line on a map that joins together places of equal pressure.
LACCOLITH	A dome-shaped igneous intrusion.
LAVA	Molten magma that erupts at the surface.
LIGHT YEAR	The distance that light travels in one year.
LIMESTONE	A sedimentary rock made of calcium carbonate.
LOAD	Eroded material transported by a river current.
MAGMA	Molten rock which exists in pockets below ground.
MAGNETOMETER	Instrument for measuring changes in the Earth's magnetism.
MANTLE	Denser layer of rock below the Earth's crust.
MARBLE	Metamorphic limestone.
MARIA	Dark basaltic lowland areas on the Moon's surface.
METAMORPHIC	Any rock changed by heat and/or pressure.
METAQUARTZITE	A metamorphosed sandstone.
METEOR	A boulder hurtling through space.
METEORITE	A meteor that hits the Earth's surface.
NAPPE	A large-scale loop fold seen in fold mountain ranges.
NEBULA	A cloud of gas and dust in space.
NORTH ATLANTIC DRIFT	see the GULF STREAM.
NUCLEAR FUSION	The release of energy caused by two atoms combining to form a new element.
ORBIT	The path of movement of one heavenly body around another in space.

ORE	A mineral deposit containing metals that are worthwhile to extract.
OOLITH	A small layered sphere of calcium carbonate.
OOLITIC LIMESTONE	A limestone composed of ooliths.
OOZE	Deep sea mud.
OZONE	An unstable form of oxygen (O_3) that absorbs harmful ultra-violet radiation from the Sun in the upper atmosphere.
PERMEABLE	A rock which allows water to pass through it.
PHOTOSPHERE	The outer layers of the Sun's atmosphere.
PILLOW LAVA	Submarine lava formed by rapid cooling.
PLACER	Mineral ores found in stream deposits.
PLATE TECTONICS	The theory that the Earth's surface is divided into a number of rigid plates that jostle each other for position.
POROUS	A rock with spaces between the grains.
PROMINENCE	A huge erupting flame of burning gases from the Sun's surface.
REGOLITH	The lunar soil.
RIFT VALLEY	A valley formed by the sinking of the crust between two normal faults.
SCHIST	A metamorphic rock with fine bands of minerals running through it.
SCREE	Loose broken rock debris at the foot of a slope.
SEA-FLOOR SPREADING	The sideways movement of new crust formed at mid-ocean ridges by igneous activity.
SEDIMENTARY	A rock produced by the settling of sediment.
SEISMIC PROSPECTING	The study of the behaviour of artificial shockwaves as they pass through underground rock layers.
SEISMOGRAM	The record of an earthquake.
SEISMOMETER	An instrument used to record earthquake shockwaves.
SHADOW ZONE	A zone where earthquake shockwaves are not detected because of refraction of shockwaves by the dense core.
SHALE	A sedimentary deposit of compacted mud.
SHIELD	A large volcano with shallow slopes; an area of very old continental crust.
SILL	A sheet intrusion that is squeezed in between the rock layers.
SLATE	Metamorphic rock formed by pressure from shale or mudstone.
SLINGSHOT EFFECT	The use of the gravity of a planet to increase the velocity of a spacecraft as it passes by.
SMOKER VENT	Hot submarine sulphide springs.
SOLAR SYSTEM	The Sun, with its orbiting planets and asteroids.
SPECIFIC GRAVITY	The relative density of a material compared to water.

SPICULE	Small eruptions of gases from the Sun's surface.
SPRING	A place where the water table reaches the surface.
STALACTITE	An icicle-like structure formed by the deposition of calcium carbonate (lime) in limestone caves.
STALAGMITE	A pillar-like structure found beneath stalactites in limestone caves formed by deposition of lime from the dripping water.
STREAK	The colour of the powder of a mineral.
SUBDUCTION	The return of a descending oceanic plate to the mantle.
SUPERNOVA	The sudden brilliant explosion of a dying star.
SYNCLINE	A downfold in a rock layer.
TECTONICS	Deforming processes caused by plate movements.
TRANSFORM FAULT	A large vertical fault separating two plates.
TRENCH	A deep gash in the ocean floor caused by a subducting plate.
TRIBUTARY	A stream which joins a larger stream.
TROPOSPHERE	The lowest layer of the Earth's atmosphere.
TSUNAMI	A large destructive seawave produced by earthquakes or volcanoes.
TURBIDITY CURRENT	A submarine avalanche.
UNCONFORMITY	The plane of an old erosion surface between older rocks below and younger rocks above.
UNIVERSE	All the space, matter and energy in existence throughout time.
VEIN	A crack in the rocks containing deposits of minerals.
VOLCANISM	Volcanic activity.
WATER CYCLE	The circulation of water through the atmosphere and the Earth's surface.
WATER TABLE	The level at which underground rocks are fully saturated with groundwater.
WATERSHED	The ridge between adjacent drainage basins.
WEATHERING	The process of decay and breakup of rocks due to the weather.